About Myself

About Myself

by
NEVIN C. HARNER

THE CHRISTIAN EDUCATION PRESS

268
H22a

28983

May '53

PRINTED IN THE UNITED STATES OF AMERICA

CONTENTS

About Myself

INTRODUCTION

The essence of all education is self-discovery and self-control. When education helps an individual to discover his own powers and limitations and shows him how to get out of his heredity its largest and best possibilities, it will fulfil its real function; when children are taught not merely to know things but particularly to know themselves, not merely how to do things but especially how to compel themselves to do things, they may be said to be really educated. For this sort of education there is demanded rigorous discipline of the powers of observation, of the reason, and especially of the will.

—From *Heredity and Environment in the Development of Man,* by EDWIN GRANT CONKLIN. Princeton University Press. Used by permission.

HAVE YOU ever lost your head ("blown your top") in a game, a meeting, or merely a chance conversation, and felt like kicking yourself afterward—and not been able to understand why in the world you flew into a temper with so little excuse?

Have you ever been moody for an hour or a day without any known reason?

Have you ever said to yourself that you were going to get down to the books this week, and then not done any better than before?

Have you ever been ill at ease, self-conscious, and generally unhappy in a group, and been unable to account for it?

Have you ever wondered how good you really were, and how much you would amount to, and what you would be doing twenty years from the present?

1

Have you ever become aware suddenly that the way you look to other people and the way you look to yourself are two quite different things, and that the impression you make is not at all what you think you are making or want to make?

In short, have you ever been a mystery to yourself?

The Person Nobody Knows

Most of us are mysteries to ourselves a good part of the time. Bruce Barton once wrote a book entitled *The Man Nobody Knows*. He was referring, of course, to Jesus; for his book was a biography of Jesus. But the person nobody really knows is himself.

The reason for this is not hard to find. It is just as difficult to understand oneself as it is to see oneself without a mirror. Has it ever occurred to you that, if there were no mirrors, you wouldn't have much idea what you look like? Primitive man must have had only the roughest notion of his own appearance. He could, of course, run his fingers over his head and face to trace their general outlines; or perhaps his wife and children were unkind enough to comment on the matter; or he might some lucky day catch a glimpse of himself in a quiet pool; but most of the time he had to guess. The only eyes you have to see with are your own eyes, and they look out rather than in. You can view others clearly, but yourself only in part—arms and legs quite well and even the tip of your nose, but forehead, cheeks, chin, neck, and back not at all. In the same way, the only mind you have with which to understand yourself is your own mind. The only feelings you have with which to "feel" yourself are your own feelings. And so you are often better at understanding others than yourself. You may know well what Bobby Burns was talking about when he wrote:

> Oh, wad some power the giftie gie us,
> To see oursels as ithers see us!

It can be a trifle embarrassing to carry around with you constantly a self that is not well understood. For one thing, you may find yourself doing things that you don't really want to do, and failing to do things that you want very much to do. For another thing, you may wake up to the fact that others see you in a different light from the way you have thought of yourself. A schoolboy was once brought up short by hearing his teacher say to him, "Don't whine so much!" He had never thought of himself as being given to whining, but apparently he had been at it for quite a while. Now all at once a mirror was held up before him, and he saw something quite different from what he expected to see.

It is a good thing every now and then (not too much or too often) to spend some time on self-understanding. The outcome should be a greater ability to make the most of oneself, and also a finer sympathy with others who are traveling along the same road.

Please Meet Yourself

The purpose of this book is really that of introducing yourself to you. It says to you, in effect: "Mr. (or Miss) So-and-so, may I present your self. You have doubtless heard a good bit about this person, but, if I am not mistaken, you have never been formally introduced. I hope very much that you two will become good friends. You will find your self to be an interesting person. As you become better acquainted, there will be many things to learn about this new acquaintance. Some of them will be quite pleasant, but others may not be, for no one is perfect. But your self is a person worth knowing. You will never regret this introduction. I venture to say that the two of you will remain inseparable throughout the rest of your life."

Our Debt to Psychology

Our grandparents knew a great deal about human nature, and their grandparents before them. In fact, you can turn to the Bible and in writings now two to three thousand years old

3

find many sound insights into what we human beings are like and why we act as we do. And a favorite saying of a very ancient Greek philosopher was, "Know thyself." But the scientific study of human nature is a very recent matter.

These lines are being written near the midpoint of the twentieth century. The science of psychology, which means "the study of the soul," got under way about the time this century began. During this brief period—less than a person's lifetime—we have probably discovered more actual facts about human nature than in all the centuries preceding.

Within these fifty years psychologists have performed literally thousands of careful experiments with people, and a great many others with animals. One great pioneer used to go into his psychological laboratory every night of the year, allowing himself only a couple of evenings a year free. Nobody made him do this, but he simply wanted to discover as much as he could about the mysteries of human nature. Other men and women have dealt patiently with thousands of cases of people who have come to them in clinics or in personal conferences, most of them persons in trouble of some sort or other. They have studied these cases, kept careful written records of them, followed them through months and years, and tried to understand their meaning. Still others have sat down with the findings of these first-hand workers and thought out the significance of it all, and then written it down in books or taught it to their pupils in classes. And thus our knowledge has grown.

There is still a great deal to learn. We know less about human nature than we do, for example, about physics or chemistry. One reason is that we began to give it serious study so recently. We could scarcely expect to learn everything there is to know in half a century. Another reason is that man represents the highest and most complicated level in all of God's creation, far more intricate and difficult to understand than the structure of an atom or the complexities of our solar system. We could scarcely expect to ferret out all the details of the

Almighty's greatest creative activity easily and perfectly. As a matter of fact, there may be much about ourselves and others that we shall never know. But we are on the way! And we owe a tremendous debt of gratitude to the patient, capable, thoughtful men and women who have brought us thus far along.

* * * * * *

The Old Testament verses quoted in this book are from the King James Version. The New Testament verses are from the Revised Standard Version of the New Testament, copyrighted, 1946, by the International Council of Religious Education, and are used by permission.

I will praise thee; for I am fearfully and wonderfully made.

1

THE RAW MATERIALS

Persons are to have our attention. They need to be freshly seen—all sorts and kinds of persons at all stages of growth: these strange two-legged creatures, erect for action or supine for sleep, clad in native hair and furs or in cut-aways or pajamas, climbing anciently out of danger into trees or modernly into danger in airplanes; creatures with beautiful supple bodies, with muscles, nerves, mysterious glands, and each with three or four quarts of miracle-working blood apiece—with eyes and ears and noses, with tongues for taste and talk, with brains and hearts, with viscera and organs of sex, with arms and legs and fingers and toes, all hung on a limber mechanical framework and covered with smooth elastic integument. . . . They are persons *with attitudes, prejudices, hopes and fears, hates and loves, hidden motivations, deep desires, and mysterious flashes of insight that dart about behind their eyes and words.*

—From *A Person-Minded Ministry,* by RICHARD HENRY EDWARDS. Abingdon-Cokesbury Press. Used by permission.

IF YOU go past a lot where a house is being built, you may see piles of bricks and sand, sacks of cement, pieces of lumber large and small, lengths of pipe and spouting, and all the other materials which go into the making of a house. When they are finally assembled, they will constitute something quite different from any or all of the various items which went into it.

In the same way your body furnishes the raw materials for your "self." There are eyes and ears, nerve cells and fibers, muscles and glands, and all the other elements which go into the making of a personality. Out of them comes something quite different from any of the separate parts, and far superior

7

to all of them taken together. The end-result is nothing less than a living soul.

Senses—Five or More

Out on the edge of the body are a number of highly specialized cells which give us our only contact with the outside world. Apart from these cells, we would have no knowledge whatsoever of what our world is like, or of what is going on out there. Some time ago a blind man was observed sitting in a theater during a dramatic production, his artificial eyes staring glassily into space. Much of what was transpiring "before his very eyes" was a complete blank to him. He could see neither lights, nor colors, nor stage scenery, nor players, nor costumes, nor his neighbors beside him—all because something had gone wrong with one set of cells through which he would normally have been in touch with the world about him. Helen Keller was deprived not merely of sight but of hearing also, so that two of the main avenues between herself and life were completely blocked. She won the unbounded admiration of all who knew her by the great courage with which she pressed forward toward a life rich and full despite her handicap. No gorgeous sunsets! No organ melodies! Nothing but touch, taste, and smell! If we were to continue to subtract these senses one by one, we should reach a point where absolutely nothing around us would register within. But fortunately most of us have all our senses intact, and receive through them countless messages from other persons and the world which is our home.

Let us begin with the eye, which in many respects is the most marvelous of all. Toward the front is a lens, which gathers up rays of light and brings them to a proper focus. In front of that is a self-adjusting opening, which narrows in the face of brilliant illumination and opens wide when the light is dim. On the back surface of the eye is the retina, the sensitive film of the eye-camera. It is made up of innumerable tiny rods and cones. The rods function at night, and do not detect color-shades but merely various degrees of brightness. You may have noticed that all objects appear to have about the same color on a moonless night. The cones, seven million of them, are operative in the daytime and register color. The optic nerves carry all of this to the rear segment of the brain, and we "see." On a perfectly clear night our eyes can pick up a matchflame two hundred miles away. But this is not the end of the story. We have two eyes, and yet we see only a single image. These twin "cameras" by an intricate and automatic adjustment of tiny muscles converge on an object near or far so that we see it once and only once, and can even tell approximately how far away it is from us.

Perhaps next in interest and importance is the apparatus by which we hear. What we call the ear is merely a framework of skin and cartilage extending out from the head a little way in order to gather up as many sound waves as possible. The real business of hearing goes on deeper within the ear. First there is the eardrum, much like any other drum except that it is very small. The eardrum vibrates with the sound waves which are caught by the outer ear and turned inward. These vibrations are carried by several tiny interlocking bones in a fluid-filled chamber, until finally they reach an instrument called the "cochlea," which means "snail" and looks for all the world like a miniature snail shell. Curled up within the cochlea is a membrane containing fibers of varying lengths. The longer ones respond to low pitched notes with slow vibrations, and the shorter ones to high pitched notes with rapid vibrations. All this, we must remember, takes place within a space no larger than a small thimble. The auditory nerves carry these impulses to the proper portion of the brain, and we "hear." What began as alternate waves of thickly compressed and thinly scattered air molecules ends up as the sound of a doorbell, an automobile horn, the clatter of falling rocks, a speaker's voice, Rachmaninoff's Prelude in C Sharp Minor, or boogie-woogie.

There is a famous story of a great musician who was trying

9

one evening to find his own house in a row of dwellings all alike. To the amazement of his companions, he simply went along kicking each successive mud-scraper, until he came to the right one. "D sharp," he said, and walked triumphantly into his home. His hearing mechanism was in very good order. But each of us, unless his ears have been damaged by disease or physical injury, has the priceless ability to hear and hear well.

Three times a day, and sometimes oftener, we utilize yet another avenue of contact with our world, the sense of taste. Within the mouth of each person are about two hundred and fifty taste buds. Food juices run down into these little buds, and we say that a thing tastes good or bad. But the matter is not so simple as it seems, for, whether we know it or not, we do different kinds of tasting in different places. There are four basic tastes, and they register in four different areas—sweet at the tip of the tongue, sour at the sides, bitter at the back, and salt at the tip and sides. If it were not for these two hundred and fifty taste buds, we would not distinguish one food from another. In old age the number of taste buds declines somewhat, which is one reason why some older people do not take as much interest in eating as they once did and do not eat enough for their own good.

Next in order is the sense of smell. Within the lining of the nose are sensitive receptors which detect various fragrances and odors, pleasant and unpleasant. Much of what we call taste is really smell, for, as we have seen, the fundamental taste-qualities are few in number. The other shades of difference among foods are in part at least detected in the nose rather than in the mouth. If you do not believe this, try eating some familiar foods while holding your nose shut. The truth is that we do part of our tasting with our noses.

Finally, there is the sense of touch, which is really not one but four distinct senses—pressure, pain, heat, and cold. Our skin is lined with microscopic pressure spots, a hundred and thirty-five to a square centimeter on the ball of the thumb and only ten in a like area on the upper arm. Pain spots number about sixty to a square centimeter on the ball of the thumb and two hundred and thirty on the neck. By and large, the pain spots far outnumber the pressure spots. Apparently it is much more important for us to be aware of something that might cause us pain than it is to detect varying degrees and types of pressure on our bodies. Heat spots are distinct from these two, and cold spots different still. Strangely enough, we feel heat in one set of spots, and cold in another.

These are the ways in which we are in contact with the world around us. Can you imagine what life would be like without them?

The Nervous System

If we were to ask, "Where does the self live and act?" the best answer we could give would be, "In the nervous system." Certainly this enormously complicated interlacing of nerve cells and fibers is much closer to the heart of personal life than our bones and muscles, or even our eyes and ears.

The unit of this system is a nerve cell, which is much like any other cell in that it is a speck of protoplasm with a nucleus at its center. At one end of the cell-body are tiny tendrils, which receive incoming "messages" or impulses. At the other end is typically a fiber or axon which may be quite short or as much as several feet long, and which ends in a little tuft of branches along which outgoing impulses pass on to the next cell. What we call a "nerve" in ordinary speech is really a cable made up of many nerve fibers. Through these cells and fibers nerve currents sweep along at varying rates of from one yard to a hundred yards a second.

There are three main divisions of the nervous system. The first consists of the sensory nerves, which are like the wires carrying incoming messages to a telephone switchboard. The second is the central nervous system, consisting chiefly of the spinal cord and the brain, which is like the telephone exchange

11

of a large city. The third consists of the motor nerves, which are like the wires carrying outgoing messages from a switch-board to innumerable points.

Of these three, by all odds the most important is the central portion of the system. It contains the almost inconceivable number of twelve billion cells, virtually all of them present when a baby is born. Carefully guarded against injury within the backbone stretches the spinal cord, with sensory and motor nerves branching off at the various joints between the verte-brae. Above this the brain is enclosed and protected within the skull-case—and well it may be protected, for here above all the life of a person centers. In man the greater part of the brain is made up of the cerebrum, which fills the major portion of the skull cavity from the forehead across the top and downward almost to the base of the neck. In the lower animals the cere-brum is less important, but in the human species it bulks large in every sense of the word. Its folded cortex ("bark") contains myriads of cells, while its interior is made up of innumerable connecting fibers running to and fro. Here we do our thinking, our remembering, our deciding, our seeing, our hearing, and the voluntary moving of our bodies.

To a degree, there is a division of labor in the cerebral cortex, and different parts do different things. You may wonder how anyone could find out what part of the brain is doing what. Well, psychologists have studied this problem through slicing away successive portions of the brains of animals, and noting the changes in their behavior with each new step. They have also learned what they could from human beings whose brains were injured by accident or disease. Knowing what part of the brain was affected, and observing what the individual could not now do at all or could not do so well as he once could, they have been able to put two and two together and draw some fairly sure conclusions as to the functions cared for in the different areas. In addition, they have experimented with mild electrical stimulation of various portions of the cortex to discover the effect upon the individual as each spot was touched.

As a result of these observations, we have some detailed knowledge of the activity of the different parts of the brain, and even of the several areas of the cerebral cortex. For example, as has already been pointed out, the sight-area lies on the surface of the rear lobe of the cerebrum, at the opposite end of the head from the eyes. The processes of thought center in the large frontal lobe. And the movement of different parts of the body—arms, legs, and the like—lies in a narrow band running from the top of the head down either side toward the ears. Strangely enough, the left side of the brain controls the right side of the body, and vice versa. In a right-handed person the left portion of the brain is slightly better developed, while in a left-handed person it is the right portion of the brain.

Farther down in the interior of the head are the older parts of the brain, which emerged first in the process of evolution. Here is the cerebellum, which has to do with maintaining body balance and carrying out complicated bodily movements such as walking and swimming. During the first year of a baby's life, which is just the time when he is learning to stand erect and coordinate his muscles for walking and jumping, the cerebellum increases four times in size. Far down in the center of the skull is another section of the old brain which serves as a very delicate thermostat for regulating the temperature of the body. If the blood running through it begins to be a trifle cool, the thermostat automatically "turns on the draft" and speeds up the body processes. If the blood becomes too warm, the thermostat slows things down. Nearby is another part which is headquarters for emotions like fear and anger. How a person can contemplate all this and not believe in God, is a little hard to see. As the verse at the opening of this chapter says, we are "fearfully and wonderfully made."

But we have not quite finished the story of the central nervous system. On each side of the spine are little clusters or ganglia of nerve cells which play a very important role in the functioning of the body and the life of the individual. On the one hand, they are connected with the spinal cord and the brain. On the other hand, motor nerves run out to organs and glands of the body. These little switchboards, while under the general overlordship of the brain, have managed to work out some independence of their own. For this reason they are called the "autonomic" nervous system (the word is much like "automatic" in both appearance and meaning). If you want to try these little switchboards out, see if you can make your heart beat faster by saying, "I will now make my heart beat faster." It doesn't work, does it? The ganglia of the autonomic system have the business well in hand.

As a matter of fact, this system really consists of two opposing divisions. The ganglia parallel to a dozen vertebrae in the middle of the spine are at work in the ordinary processes of life, such as eating, digestion, sexual activity, and the like. The ganglia above and below this central section are operative in the extraordinary emergencies of life, such as a slap in the face which makes us angry, or a ten-ton truck bearing down on us which frightens us. And these two divisions work in exact opposition to each other. The middle section, for example, promotes the flow of a good supply of blood to the digestive tract (because that is what the body needs at the time of a good Thanksgiving dinner); while the end sections reduce the flow of blood to the digestive tract when a stiff fight is in the offing (because what the individual needs at that moment is not to digest his dinner but to have the muscles of back, arms, and legs in excellent working order). And so the two shuttle back and forth, equipping us for both the ordinary and the extraordinary happenings of life in a truly marvelous manner.

Muscles and Glands

An outgoing message from the central nervous system may end, and often does, in the fibers of a muscle. For instance, if you touch a sharp point lightly to a baby's hand, the nerve

14

impulse will rush inward from the pain spots to the central system; in a case like this, it may not get much higher than the spinal cord; back comes the motor impulse to the muscles of the arm; and the hand is pulled away out of danger. When the baby is a couple of years older and his cerebrum is functioning better, the message may go all the way to the top level of the brain, and he may do some thinking about the matter while he jerks his hand away. "What is going on here? Why is that person sticking me with a pin? Why should I have to take this lying down?" And the muscles of the arm may not merely pull the hand away from the pin, but also double up the hand into a fist and poke you in the face if you are down on the child's level. This is one way the motor part of the nervous system operates.

But an outgoing message may end also in an organ, such as the stomach, or in a gland. In this case, the impulse will probably detour through the autonomic system which we have just considered. For our present purpose, we need not say much about the organs, but the glands are a different matter. Some of them are very important, especially the ones that have no ducts but discharge their secretions directly into the blood stream. They are called endocrine glands (meaning "secreting internally"); they are all tied up with the autonomic nervous system; and they have a great deal to do with our emotional life and something to do with the development of our personalities. Let us look at a few of the more interesting ones.

Squarely in the center of the head lies a gland about the size of a pea which is called the pi-tú-i-tar-y. This little bundle of tissue has the important function of regulating the growth of the bony skeleton. If it begins to become overactive in infancy, the result is a giant; if underactive, the result is a dwarf. Many of the sideshows at circuses would have to go out of existence if it were not for this gland. But this is not all, for the pituitary is a very versatile fellow. It also has the task of stimulating the activity of other glands, some of which we shall mention soon.

15

For this reason it has been called "the conductor of the endocrine orchestra." From its central vantage point in the head, it waves its baton and steps up the activity of one gland or another, much as the conductor of an orchestra calls now for a little more volume from the brass section, and again for more activity from the woodwinds.

In the throat lies a purplish gland, with which we are probably more familiar, called the thyroid. When it becomes enlarged, we know it as a goiter. This gland regulates how fast the body "burns" food to create heat and energy. In other words, it is the furnace draft of the body. When it is overactive, the person is likely to be thin, wiry, high-strung, and nervous—very much like a fire that is burning vigorously with the draft wide open. When it is underactive, the pulse rate goes down, the mind doesn't work quite so well, the person grows fat (because food is not turned into energy but simply lies around inert in the body), sluggish, and tired—very much like a fire that is almost out. The secretion of the thyroid is about two-thirds iodine. People living near the seashore get a proper amount of iodine in their food, but others living far inland must eat iodized salt in order to avoid goiters and disturbances of the thyroid gland.

Much farther down in the body, atop the kidneys, lie two yellowish glands which are called the adrenals. (The word means simply "near the kidneys.") The inner core of the adrenal glands is a tiny factory for the secretion of adrenalin, a most powerful drug. One writer has calculated that a row of street sprinklers twenty miles long, with two hundred sprinklers to the mile and each one containing six hundred and twenty-five gallons, would supply just enough water to weaken one ounce of pure adrenalin to the right strength for body use. The adrenals are the emergency glands of the body. We might almost call them the Department of Personal Defense.

When we become angry or afraid, adrenalin pours into the body, and a great many things happen all at once. The heart speeds up. (Have you ever felt your heart pounding when you got angry or when you stood before a large audience to make a speech?) The blood pressure rises. Sugar is released from the liver to provide additional energy. Digestion slows down or stops entirely, for the reason that, when a dinosaur or a ten-ton truck is approaching, the important thing is not to digest a recent meal but to get away—and fast! (This is why a person may have a spell of indigestion after a quarrel at the dinner table.) The breathing rate increases, so as to insure an adequate supply of oxygen. The blood that is drawn away from the digestive tract is channeled into the large muscles of the body, where it will do the most good for fighting or running. At the same time it is drained out of the surface blood vessels. (This is the explanation of a person's paleness when he is "scared white.") The subject is now less likely to bleed to death if wounded, especially since adrenalin helps to coagulate the blood. In animals, such as a cat, the hair stands on end to make the intended victim seem larger and more formidable. There may be a relic of this even in humans in the prickly skin which we call "goose flesh." Thus in a variety of ways the whole organism adapts itself to a crisis.

These adjustments were quite helpful in getting primitive man out of the reach of a saber-toothed tiger. They are still useful in many modern emergencies, such as an automobile accident. A passenger may be able to lift one end of the car to free a badly wounded person, whereas an hour before he would not have been able to budge it. Unfortunately, the same procedure goes on its tireless way when a concert pianist appears on the stage for the first time. His body is still back in the forests of the Old World, trying to get away from that tiger. But the adjustments which once saved many a life now merely serve to make the pianist miserable. Perhaps in fifty thousand years from now our adrenals will have caught up with the requirements of civilized life.

One more set of glands deserves our attention—the sex

glands. In addition to their task of manufacturing the reproductive cells which have the power of starting a new life, they also pour certain secretions directly into the blood stream. These change the boy's body into a man's, and the girl's into a woman's. The reproductive organs develop rapidly at the time of puberty. The boy's voice drops an octave, his beard begins to grow, and his muscles become large and strong. The girl likewise becomes a woman, whose body is quite different both in appearance and in function from what it was five years before. From puberty to the change of life in middle age the sex glands are most active, and it is precisely these years in which the sexes differ most from each other. Before puberty, in childhood, boys and girls look and act very much the same. And again in old age a man's voice may become high and squeaky and his body rounded and womanish, while a woman may begin to grow hair on her face and become square and angular in body. Obviously, the sex glands not only prepare the way for the next generation, but also have much to do with the life of this one.

All of these glands, and others which could be mentioned, interact and cooperate. At puberty, when the sex glands step up their activity, the harmony seems to be upset for the time being. It is almost as though a scale were carefully balanced after long effort, and then a ten-pound weight were suddenly dumped on the one pan. At any rate, the basal metabolism rate, which tells how fast the body is turning food into energy, generally goes up about thirteen or fourteen points just before puberty starts. It is little wonder that teen-agers sometimes don't quite know whether they are going or coming.

The endocrine glands are very much influenced by the way we feel. When we become angry, our adrenal glands go into high gear. And if we worry too long and too hard, the bodily effect is so marked (through the endocrine glands, in part) that we may develop stomach ulcers. But the opposite is also true, namely, the endocrine glands can influence the way we feel.

18

If they are not working as they should, we may become irritable and nervous, or moody and depressed. All of life seems to be tied up in one bundle, and everything affects everything else sooner or later.

The Finished Product

Out of these raw materials your "self" arises. Many experiences are undergone which register in your nervous system, many acts are performed, many habits are acquired. These little bits of personality are woven together into larger units—love for home, loyalty to country, devotion to church, as well as some tendencies perhaps toward meanness, selfishness, and dishonesty. These in turn are interlaced into a person, a self, which can look down upon the raw materials out of which it has been built up; which can think long, long thoughts; which can remember the past, live well in the present, and dream of the future. Is it strange that we speak of man as being made in the image of God?

The fathers have eaten a sour grape, and the children's teeth are set on edge.

—JEREMIAH 31:29

2

CHIP OFF THE OLD BLOCK

"Where have I come from, where did you pick me up?"
the baby asked its mother.

She, half crying, half laughing, and clasping the baby to her breast,—

"You were hidden in my heart as its desire, my darling.

"In all my hopes and my loves, in my life, in the life of my mother, you have lived.

"In the lap of the deathless Spirit who rules our home you have been nursed for ages.

"Heaven's first darling, twin-born with the morning light, you have floated down the stream of the world's life, and at last you have stranded on my heart.

"As I gaze on your face, mystery overwhelms me: you who belong to all have become mine.

"For fear of losing you I hold you tight to my breast. What magic has snared the world's treasure in these slender arms of mine?"

—From *The Crescent Moon*, by RABINDRANATH TAGORE. Copyright 1913 by The Macmillan Company and used with their permission. "The Beginning."

WE KNOW well the meaning of the phrase which heads this chapter. Just as a chip contains the same wood of the same color and texture and grain as the block from which it has come, so a boy is like his father in looks and acts and abilities and a girl is like her mother. More accurately, a boy bears a mixed resemblance to both of his parents, and so does a daughter.

Is this true? If so, why is it true? In what respects is it true? How true is it? Are you fairly free to develop along any line you choose, and to make of yourself pretty much what you want? Or was it already determined before your birth what you now are, and what you are likely to become?

Why Are Babies Like Their Parents?

On first thought, this may seem like a foolish question, in the same class as the old joker, "Why is the ocean so near the shore?" But, on second thought, it becomes amazingly difficult to answer. Granted for the moment that a baby gets the color of its eyes by inheritance, how does this come about? When the embryo is first of all a tiny speck in the mother's body, and then the size of an acorn, and later still a few inches long, what makes the eyes of this new individual take on one shade of color rather than another? In order to find the answer, we must delve into the process by which a new life starts and grows. There is much here which we do not know as yet, but on some points we can be fairly certain.

As everyone is aware, a baby results from the fusion of a sperm and an egg, coming respectively from the father and from the mother. Let us center our thought principally on the sperm, although what we say of it is equally true of the egg, except that the latter is larger.

A sperm is infinitesimally small. It would take almost half a trillion to weigh a pound (a trillion is a million times a million). At the heart of the sperm is a nucleus four ten-thousandths of an inch in diameter. Inside this nucleus are twenty-four pairs of chromosomes, which may be likened to strings of beads. Each chromosome contains some hundreds of beads, which are called genes—perhaps thirty thousand or so in all. Each bead is always in the same string, and at the same place in that string. For example, bead No. 279 in chromosome No. 17 never shows up at some other spot; it is always right where it ought to be. Before fertilization takes place, every sperm divides into two cells, each of which contains twenty-four chromosomes instead of twenty-four pairs. The egg does the same, so that when the two unite the new

21

bones of the infant that is to be? And when cell multiplication starts in the embryo, why do some cells develop into a brain, while others develop into a leg? There is much here which is utterly mysterious; and the greater mystery is how anyone can think on such matters and not believe in God.

Some Things We Inherit

As has been implied already, it is pretty clear that we inherit our bodily characteristics from our ancestors. This is not to say that a child looks exactly like either its father or its mother. For one-half of its inheritance comes from each of its parents, one-fourth from each of its grandparents, one-eighth from each of its great-grandparents, and so back through history. Every baby is the meeting-point of a number of hereditary streams, and no one is exactly like any other person who ever lived. Nevertheless, it still remains true that the color of your eyes was fixed by the genes at the moment your separate life began, and there is nothing you can do about it. You cannot, by exercising will power, change your eyes to another color. Nor will attending another school, or moving to another state, or happiness, or sorrow, or any other experience alter their shading in the least. That was fixed a number of years ago by the slender strings of beads about which we have been thinking; and so were the other major characteristics of your body.

Beyond this, it seems fairly clear that intelligence is determined largely by heredity. By intelligence we do not mean how much a person happens to know at any given moment. That is knowledge. Rather we mean a person's sheer ability to learn; his quickness to get new facts; his alertness to a new situation which he has never met before; his general level of brightness. And this seems to come down to him pretty largely through the genes.

In a matter of so great importance, you have a right to ask how we know this, or how we arrive at this conclusion. The matter has been studied by a great many people from a variety

24

of angles. One approach has been to make a careful comparison between ordinary children growing up in their own homes and adopted children growing up in foster homes. The former are influenced by their parents in two ways, namely, environment and heredity. They live with their parents, hear them talk, follow their example, read the books and magazines they provide; but they are also the blood-descendants of their parents. The latter are influenced by their foster parents in one way only, namely, environment. When the statistics show that true children are much more like their parents in point of intelligence than foster children are, it begins to look as though heredity had a good deal to do with shaping intelligence.

Another approach has been to follow the I.Q. (Intelligence Quotient) of children through successive years and some changes in environment, to see whether it changes or remains very much the same. (The Intelligence Quotient is found by dividing the mental age which a person reveals on an intelligence test by his actual age. If he has a mental age of seven when he is actually ten years old, his I.Q. is 70. On the other hand, if he has a mental age of thirteen ten years after birth, his I.Q. is 130.) Many observations of this sort have been conducted. In some cases, they have involved orphans taken out of homes with little or nothing in the way of books, music, or intellectual stimulation and placed with families providing everything necessary to make intelligence grow—if it will grow at all. In other cases, the children have been moved in the opposite direction, that is, from good homes to poor homes. The results are not entirely clear. In certain instances the I.Q. has gone up or down a good bit; but by and large it has not changed greatly. Fluctuations of five or ten points are quite common, but larger changes are not. This, too, begins to look as though the level of intelligence were fixed principally by the genes. Good home, poor home; good school, poor school— these may cause the I.Q. to shift somewhat in some persons, but comparatively little in most, and not at all in many.

Several good psychologists, after weighing the evidence carefully, have come out at the conclusion that differences in intelligence among individuals are about four-fifths due to heredity, and about one-fifth due to environment or experience. Perhaps that is as good a way as any to leave the matter.

Beyond physical characteristics and intelligence, there seems to be little that we inherit from our parents. We may have to leave a place in our thinking for the inheritance of certain special talents, such as exceptional musical ability. There are some cases which are very hard to account for otherwise. The great musician Mozart, for example, even in childhood could name any note which he heard, and readily learned to play various instruments skillfully without a teacher. He started to compose at the age of four, began to give his own recitals at seven, and wrote his first opera by the time he was thirteen. Even though his father was a talented composer, and the boy grew up with music all around him, it is hard to explain such outstanding genius without falling back upon the genes, the carriers of heredity. Or consider the case of Blind Tom, who astounded many audiences a few generations ago. Without training, without normal intelligence, and without vision, he could play any piece he heard, reproducing even the mistakes. In music, then, and perhaps in other fields such as art or mathematics, it may be that special talent is passed on from one generation to another by heredity.

Some Things We Don't Inherit

The preceding section leaves out many matters, thereby implying that everything else within us comes not through heredity but as the outcome of experience. This is certainly taking a great deal for granted. Let us, therefore, examine some of these other matters.

There is good reason for believing that we do not inherit our characters from our parents, either good or bad. Ofttimes we assume that the opposite is true. One summer morning after the offering is taken in vacation school, we find that money is missing from the collection plate. The theft is finally traced to a ten-year-old boy, who has long been under suspicion. Our first impulse may be to say: "Well, what would you expect? His father has been jailed twice for robbery, and is now out on probation. Blood will out! Like father, like son." And there we are tempted to leave the case, feeling that everything has been explained satisfactorily. But the explanation is too easy. It leaves too many things out of consideration. The boy has had the example of his father, whom he may respect and love, dangling constantly before him. Furthermore, he may have fallen in with the wrong gang, a gang in which stealing was a common and ordinary thing. Or he may have had less money and fewer toys than other boys around him, and taken to stealing as the easiest way of evening things out. In any case, whatever made him steal, it was probably not heredity. Rather he learned to steal, just as others have learned in the course of their lives to be honest.

As a matter of fact, we can see character made and unmade before our very eyes. As the years go by, a good person sometimes becomes bad, and a bad person sometimes turns good. There is nothing here which goes its own steady way regardless of circumstances, as eye-color does, or even as intelligence does. This looks like environment and experience, not heredity. Could you teach a six-year-old child to steal if you set your mind to it—any child? Probably so, if you consistently ridiculed him for having such poor clothes, and so few toys, and so little money to spend, and then left a couple of dollar bills in plain sight where he could take them easily. By the same token, you could arrange the circumstances of a child's life so that in all probability he would grow up as honest as the day is long.

To go on, there is good reason for believing that we are not born with any kind of ready-made temperament—moody, cheerful, hotheaded, or any other that could be mentioned. Again we often assume that the opposite is the case. Here is a girl in

27

a youth fellowship whose bright, sunny disposition is admired by all. We may be inclined to say: "What else would you expect? Her mother is the life of the party in any group where she is found. She inherited her mother's disposition, as sure as you are living." But again our explanation omits too many important considerations. The daughter may indeed have got her cheerful temperament in part from her mother, but there are other ways of doing this than through the genes. She has lived with her mother all her life. She has obviously been part of a happy home. Perhaps the same things that contributed to her mother's disposition—a good husband (and father), a pleasant house and surroundings, a steady income, and good health—have contributed to her disposition also.

There is a chance, just a chance, that we inherit temperamental tendencies by way of the endocrine glands. They seem to have a good deal to do with emotional make-up, and it is just possible that one person inherits a larger or a smaller thyroid or pituitary than another person. But we know so little about this, and there are so many other ways of accounting for differences in disposition that it is safer to conclude these are learned in the course of our daily experiences. One person may grow up under favorable circumstances, and become cheerful, steady, and even-tempered. Another may grow up under unfavorable circumstances, and become sulky, suspicious, and quick-tempered. Either one may change considerably in a five-year period if the circumstances change. Could you, if you wished to do so, make a child ugly-tempered? How would you go at it? Could you make him sweet-tempered? How would you go at that?

To go further, there is sufficient reason for believing that what we call insanity is probably not inherited. Every now and then an unhappy person may be seized by the fear that it is transmitted through heredity. If a close relative has been committed to an institution, the reaction may be: "I may be next. This thing is in the blood stream of our family, and I'm on the list." Here we must proceed with some care, because psychologists differ in their conclusions. Some good students of the matter speak as though mental illness, or at least a tendency in that direction, were passed on from one generation to another through the genes. But equally good students take the opposite point of view, and there is impressive evidence to support this more hopeful conclusion. By way of example, there are many cases of children whose parents have been declared insane but who have themselves lived normal and wholesome lives. Some indeed have broken down, but their illness often represented another type from that of the father or mother. Furthermore, they have often had to live in a home which was unhappy and unnatural, and they have often been hounded by the fear of what might happen to them. Such experiences alone are enough to cause some people to break under the strain.

Strange as it seems, mental illness may perhaps be best thought of as a way of life which has been learned in the course of very difficult circumstances. An "insane" person has generally gone through a great deal of anxiety and insecurity, beginning quite often in early childhood. In the course of time, he got further and further out of touch with real life, and withdrew into a private world of his own. Finally, he reached the point where he could no longer fit well into the normal round of ordinary life, and was placed in the special care of an institution created for that purpose. If the course of his life had been different, he might have lived out his days in happiness and usefulness. We cannot be absolutely sure of this interpretation, but we certainly are not sure of its opposite. And there is no point in fearing what might be true, but probably isn't.

One more thing may be noted as probably belonging not to heredity but to experience, namely, differences in ability or disposition between boys and girls. We sometimes assume that girls naturally take more to literature and art, while boys naturally are better at science and mathematics. Or we take for granted that women are naturally gentler and more tenderhearted, while men are naturally more cruel and aggressive. These assumptions are probably not true. Many men have been excellent authors and artists and musicians, and quite a few women have excelled as scientists and mathematicians. Similarly, some men are as gentle as anyone could wish, and some women can be altogether cruel.

It is unmistakably true that when we look at the two sexes in our civilization, some of these differences do actually exist. But the point is, Are they inborn? Begin with the fact that the bodies of men are taller, heavier, and better muscled than the bodies of women; what effect would this have on the personalities of the sexes over a period of five or ten thousand years? Suppose that the situation had been reversed for the past few thousand years; what then? Continue with the fact that the life-experiences of the two sexes have been quite different for many centuries. The men have fared abroad to hunt and fight and make a living; the women have stayed at home to bear the children, rear them, and make a home. What effect would this have? Add the further fact that our society expects boys to act in one way and girls to act in another; and no girl wants to be called a tomboy, and no boy wishes to be known as a sissy. What effect would this have? No, there are differences between the sexes, but they too—like so many other things—are probably learned, in major part at least. In fact, there are primitive tribes where both men and women are meek and mild; others where both are bold and self-reliant; and still others where the women are businesslike, while the men are cultured and sensitive. There is nothing in human nature which prevents a football captain from taking delight in carrying a toy to a sick child at Christmas, or a doll-faced girl from standing on her own feet and meeting life courageously.

What Difference Does It Make?

We have drawn a number of conclusions concerning what we do or do not inherit. What do they mean for us personally? Let us set down a few practical implications in rapid-fire order.

If bodily characteristics are inherited, our best chance of insuring good bodies for our children comes at the time of choosing a husband or a wife. The one family-strain which will pass on to the next generation through us is already fixed. We can do little about it except to keep it clean. But the other family-strain lies within our choice. Tall or short, thin or fat, strong or weak—it will have fifty per cent of the "say" in determining the physical make-up of our children.

If intelligence is mainly inherited, our best opportunity to insure good minds for our children comes at the point of choosing a husband or a wife. The question is not primarily whether the other person and his or her relatives have all gone to college, but rather, whether they are bright, keen, alert, adaptable, doing well whatever they do. This other set of genes will enter just as much as our own into the making of our children's intelligence.

Even if our intelligence is largely fixed by heredity, we need not become fatalistic about it. For one thing, most of us do not make the maximum use of the intelligence we have. There is no point in sighing idly for more, until we have utilized to the full what we do have. For another, the measurable change in I.Q. that apparently can be made is worth making. There is ample reason for doing consistent study, reading good literature, attending the best movies and plays, and going around with people who are mentally awake.

If character is not inherited, we can take heart. We were not foredoomed at birth or before to any degree of goodness or badness. The sky is the limit. As far as heredity goes, God in his infinite mercy has given every baby unlimited opportunity to become the best that he can be.

If temperament is not inherited, we can face the future courageously in this respect also. Are there emotional twists within us which are undesirable? They can be changed. We were probably not born that way. Change will not be easy, and

31

it surely can't be achieved overnight, but it can happen here.

If insanity is probably not inherited, we can dispel any needless fears that may have assailed us.

If personality differences between the sexes are not necessarily inborn, the best that either man or woman has achieved is open to each one of us.

In short, through heredity God seems to have endeavored to give us what was most needful, while at the same time in certain essentials leaving the door of spiritual growth wide open before us.

Train up a child in the way he should go: and when he is
old, he will not depart from it.

—PROVERBS 22: 6

3

THE LADDER OF GROWTH

We are climbing Jacob's ladder,
We are climbing Jacob's ladder,
We are climbing Jacob's ladder,
Soldiers of the cross.

Every round goes higher, higher,
Every round goes higher, higher,
We are climbing Jacob's ladder,
Soldiers of the cross.

Climbing up from earth to heaven,
Climbing up from earth to heaven,
We are climbing Jacob's ladder,
Soldiers of the cross.

WE ARE thinking here not of body-growth, but rather of
personality-growth. A little baby is far from a finished
product. As he lies in his crib a few days after birth, he is not
as yet a full-fledged person; instead he has been aptly described
as a candidate for personality. He has no character, good, bad,
or indifferent. He hardly shows as yet any real disposition,
either pleasant or unpleasant. He possesses no skills: he can't
play a piano, run a typewriter, carry a football. He is moved
by no strong feelings about the Jews, the Negroes, the Cau-
casians, the Russians, the Church, or anything else of larger
significance. He finds no meaning whatever at this stage in the
three-letter word "God." He can't think. He can't walk. He
can't talk. He can't even sit erect.

Fifty years later he will have grown up in all these respects. How does he go from here to there? What are the successive rounds in the ladder of growth? The process may look like a mere hit-or-miss affair, but it isn't that at all. On the contrary, it follows a regular and orderly course from start to finish.

The Life Story of a Habit

A baby has no habits. He has reflexes, which are simple sensory-motor patterns like the blinking of the eye when the light strikes it, but no habits. He has bodily needs and hungers, such as the "desire" to be pleasantly warm and full of food, but no habits. He has some of the raw materials essential to the building of habits, but no habits as yet. For a habit is a learned way of acting, feeling, or thinking. An adult includes hundreds and thousands of them in his personality make-up, but a baby none at all. How does an adult learn his many habits? How are habits formed? The answer comprises two basic principles which are among the most important formulations in all psychology.

The first is *the principle of practice,* which means simply that we form a habit by practicing the same thing over and over again. Let us leave the little baby far behind, and skip over a number of years to find a good example, namely, a high school student learning the touch system on a typewriter. When he first looks down at the four banks of keys, they seem to be nothing but a confused jumble of letters, numerals, and signs. But he goes over them in his mind time after time, and he also goes over them with his fingers. He may begin with simple words which utilize only a few basic letters, and add others one at a time until the whole set of keys is literally at his finger tips. He now knows that "r" lies under the first finger of the left hand on the third row of keys, and "k" under the second finger of the right hand on the second row of keys. Even his fingers know this; indeed they may know it better than his conscious mind. And he can strike these many keys in proper sequence with a speed which one would scarcely believe if he had not actually seen it.

Apparently something is present in his nervous system which wasn't there before. Impulses have traveled over the very same routes so often that they have beaten a path, as it were. It is a little like walking across a ploughed field time after time in the same course until a path is laid down. Of course, there is no change in the nerve cells or fibers which can be seen with the eye or even with a microscope. It is possible that the little tendrils and branches have grown a trifle closer to one another along these routes; or else that the nerve tissue has changed imperceptibly so that an impulse makes its way more easily the fiftieth time than it did the first; but these are only guesses, of which no one is sure. But one thing is sure: something new has been added to his nervous system, and to him. He may not touch a typewriter for five years, but when his fingers shape themselves over the keyboard again they will begin to "feel" the letters at the right places.

This is the way all habits, without exception, are formed. Has our infant in the span of four or five years become a cry-baby, bursting into tears on the slightest provocation? He has done this so often that the tracks are there, ready to be used, whenever a difficulty arises. Does a person as he walks along set one foot before the other without thinking about it, and without knowing how he does it? He has walked so much that walking has become "second nature." Does a man in business turn aside from a chance to pull a shady deal almost automatically? He has practiced this sort of honesty so long and so often that he can scarcely do anything else. Does a girl on a Sunday morning feel an almost irresistible impulse to put on her best clothes and start to church when she hears the bells ringing? She has done this so many Sundays that churchgoing is an inescapable part of her. This is the first principle of habit formation: "We learn what we practice."

The second is *the principle of satisfaction,* which means

simply that we form a habit more quickly and easily when the practice of it is accompanied by satisfaction. This should not be too hard to comprehend. When a certain way of acting, thinking, or feeling is enjoyable, we are likely to do it again. Thus we practice it more often. In part, the principle of satisfaction is as simple as that. But there may be something more! It is possible that, when a pleasant feeling-tone goes with an act, the nerve tissue is actually changed through endocrine gland secretions or in some other way, so that fewer runs or trials are required to "beat a path" than would otherwise be the case. Here again we are in the realm of guesswork, but we do know that habits form better when they are practiced with satisfaction.

Take learning to go to church as an example. It isn't enough just to be there fifty-two Sundays a year. If we have disliked it every time, we'll quit going the first Sunday we are old enough to be independent of our parents and to do what we really want to do. But if we found some enjoyment in it—the music, the sermon, the windows, being with people we like, or the quiet contentment which seems to belong to this holy place—that is different! We are likely to form a habit of church attendance which will stay with us as long as we live. "We learn what we practice with satisfaction"—this is the full statement. There are no words in psychology more important than these seven.

Every habit takes shape in accordance with these two principles; we can depend upon it. Are we in the habit of telling lies, white or otherwise, on occasion? The explanation is that we have practiced telling lies, white or otherwise, a good many times, and that the experience proved generally satisfactory. Would we like to become the kind of person who does his homework faithfully? The way to move in that direction is to settle down regularly to the books evening after evening, and hunt around for something pleasant therein—the satisfaction of doing a workmanlike job, or of discovering something new, or of pleasing one's parents, or even of getting a good report card. Do we find ourselves running around with the gang a good deal, and getting quite a kick out of it? We are well on the way to becoming a definite kind of person, the kind who lives principally for running around with the gang. And so on with all we do, think, feel, know, and are!

This discussion of habits raises one question which is worth following up a bit. Do you by any chance have a habit which is distasteful to you, and which you have often thought you would like to shake off? It may be smoking, biting your finger nails, swearing, or something else more or less serious. The question is, How did you ever happen to form a habit distasteful to you, if it is true that we learn what we practice with satisfaction? And why do you keep on doing it now? The answer is quite simple. The habit brought some satisfaction to some part of you, or you would never have learned it. And it continues to bring you some satisfaction, or you would not keep on doing it. The top part of you may find it altogether unpleasant, but farther down in your nature you are getting something out of the habit. The thing to do, then, is to inquire what satisfaction the habit is bringing you, and see if there may not be some other and better way of securing a like satisfaction. Only when you have done this will you make much headway in breaking the habit.

Likes and Dislikes

Our concern under this heading of "Likes and Dislikes" is not with the little ones, such as a fondness for oysters or a distaste for olives. We are thinking of the big ones, such as have to do with family, school, church, Negroes, Japanese, labor unions, and the like. These major likes and dislikes are called attitudes. They are not opinions. They are not judgments. They are primarily feelings. They lie in the realm of the emotions. And they are most important! In large part they make us what we are. And in equally large part they make the world what it is. War and peace, hatred and brotherhood, misery and happiness are in their hands.

37

Where do these attitudes come from? How do they creep into our lives to color our personalities so deeply, and, when multiplied by a million, to shape the course of world history?

Basically, they develop in the same way as any other habit, because attitudes are nothing but emotional habits. They are habitual ways of feeling about something. And so we learn our attitudes by practicing them with satisfaction. If our home life has been mainly happy, and we have frequently felt a deep sense of attachment to the home and all it stands for, and found satisfaction in feeling this way, we build up in time a tremendous loyalty to our home. Let someone say a word against it, and he has us to reckon with. The house is the finest house, the yard the finest yard, the furnace the finest furnace, and the people the finest people that anyone ever saw. That's the way we feel about it, and that's the way it is. By way of contrast, if during World War II we read a great deal about Japanese atrocities, and on a good many occasions indulged in letting ourselves go against the Japanese and took quite a bit of satisfaction in feeling that way, we come out after a while with a deep-seated prejudice against the Japanese. As far as we are concerned, there is not one good thing about them—no, not one! Their appearance is not attractive, their characters are not trustworthy, their land is not beautiful, their products are not worth having. We simply don't like the Japanese, and that settles the matter. In both of these instances, the attitude is clearly an emotional habit of long standing, built up in the same way as other habits, and now working automatically as all habits do. It is very much like a Jack-in-the-box. Press the spring, and out it pops.

While this is perhaps the chief way in which attitudes develop, there is another way of accounting for them which is quite helpful. When two things reach us wrapped up in the same package, as it were, we often come to feel toward the second the way we originally felt toward the first. For example, none of us like to be unpopular. If we find ourselves unpopular at school, laughed at and never elected to office, we may develop a revulsion against school itself. The two—unpopularity and school—have been so closely interwoven in our experience that we transfer to the second a feeling which was originally directed against the first. We may not be aware that this is happening, but it goes on just the same. This transfer is called "emotional conditioning." We might put its meaning this way: The direction our emotions take is shaped by conditions. A simple illustration may be found in our fear of lightning. The chances are that we were really afraid of the thunder to begin with, because a loud noise is one of the best stimuli for getting a startled reaction in children. But thunder is always accompanied by lightning. Every time we shrank in fear from thunder, a certain condition was present, namely, thunder and lightning together. So in due time the transfer was made, and we became afraid of the lightning. The emotion of fear now took a new direction and was attached to a new object because of this condition.

Many of our attitudes have all too clearly been formed by a process of emotional conditioning. Let us say that in childhood we were bored by church services. We dislike being bored. And so in time we dislike church. Or suppose that one time when we were quite small we were frightened by a Negro, whose unfamiliar face and huge frame towered high above us. Anything big and strange is likely to inspire fear in a child. The whole experience was most unpleasant. We were frightened, and perhaps we were ashamed because we were frightened. And so we wake up one day in adulthood finding ourselves bitterly but unreasonably turned against Negroes. The emotion which we once felt toward a large, strange object has now been directed against a whole people.

One more way of explaining how attitudes begin in the individual life deserves some mention. In a great many cases they are caught from the people we live with. They come to us like measles—by contagion. They sweep over a mass of people like any other epidemic. If our parents and friends all hate and mistrust the Russians, so do we. We have never given much thought to the matter. We have not inquired carefully whether or not the Russians deserve to be hated and mistrusted. Everybody's doing it, and so do we. If everyone around us stands up when the Star Spangled Banner is played, and takes off his hat when the flag passes in parade, and in general shows a deep loyalty to our country, we too stand up and take off our hats and become as patriotic as they are. It may be that we have thought the matter through and arrived at this position out of deep conviction; but more likely than not we simply go along with the crowd.

If these are the ways in which attitudes become a part of us, several rather disturbing conclusions follow. One is that there is no assurance any attitude is telling us the truth about the institution or the people concerned. As we have seen, it may be a mere habit, or the outcome of chance conditions, or a thoughtless borrowing from others. As such, it is not clearly thought through. It is not based upon carefully gathered evidence. It is simply a feeling-tone, an emotional leaning toward or away from someone or something. How sure can you be at this moment that your attitudes toward school, or church, or America, or capitalism, or the Chinese tell you the truth, the whole truth, and nothing but the truth?

Another conclusion is that an attitude is a lazy, inaccurate way of meeting any given situation. If a person is down on the Negroes, he has a ready-made way of dealing with any Negro he meets. He doesn't have to think about the matter. He doesn't have to inquire whether this particular Negro is good or bad, well-educated or illiterate, and work out an approach that fits this individual representative of the race. No, he has a pat approach for the entire race. Push the button, and out pops the Jack-in-the-box. If a person has a fixed prejudice against the Russians, he lumps them all together and treats them all alike. Now there are Russians, and Russians; but that doesn't

40

matter to an attitude. No accuracy of discrimination! No selective judgment! Just a general broadside against all Russians!

It is clear—is it not?—that attitudes are tricky affairs. Every now and then each of us ought to drag his private supply out into the light, and give it a good overhauling in the light of all the facts he can get and all the Christian principles he can discover.

Thinking Things Through

As a general rule, we don't think—that is, really think—unless and until we have to. For true thinking means finding the solution to a problem, or the way through some difficulty. Unfortunately we use the word "think" in a variety of ways in ordinary speech. We may say, "I thought and I thought, but I couldn't recall her name." Properly speaking, that is not thinking at all. It is merely remembering, or trying to remember. Or some sunshiny day we may have drifted off into a mental haze speculating pleasantly on what we would do if we suddenly came into an inheritance of a million dollars. Before our mind's eye moves a splendid procession of mansions, automobiles, yachts, fur coats, and golf clubs. Suddenly an unexpected visitor asks what we are doing, and we reply, "Oh, I was just thinking." That isn't real thinking. It is merely day-dreaming. In the true sense of the term, thinking is problem-solving.

Let us suppose that one day you are driving along a country road in an automobile, a sleek, up-to-the-minute convertible. All at once the engine gives a wheeze and a cough, and stops dead. What do you do? Well, you may pass through a brief period of what might be called mild shock. This is so unexpected. You have to shift your mental gears to take in this sudden, drastic change in the situation. A moment ago you were freewheeling along without a care in the world. Now you are motionless and helpless. But soon you begin to assemble your wits, and face things as they are.

Probably your first move is to diagnose the problem, which

means that you try to discover where the difficulty lies. How well you do this will depend on how much you know about automobiles. If your knowledge is scanty, your diagnosis may not get much further than an ineffectual "Oh dear, what can the matter be?" But if you are pretty well posted on what takes place under the hood, your diagnosis is considerably better. Is the engine overheated? A car will stop sometimes if the engine temperature mounts too high. No, the thermometer registers only normal temperature. Could it be a broken fuel pump? No, it couldn't be that, for the pump was repaired week before last by a good mechanic. Maybe it's out of gas. Sure enough, the gas gauge stands at "Empty." The day was nice, and the sun was high, and you had lost all track of distance. And so you are out of gas. The problem is diagnosed. You know where the trouble lies.

Your next step, then, is to cast about for solutions of the problem. Is there a farmhouse nearby which might have an extra supply of gasoline? Yes, there is one over there at the foot of the hill, but there are no cars, tractors, or trucks in sight. The prospects are rather poor. It's hardly worth a walk down the lane to find out. Perhaps a passing motorist will be kind enough to stop and allow some gas to be siphoned out of his tank. But, on second thought, that's not such a good idea. In the past ten miles you haven't met a single car, and the chances are against you. Could there be a gas station not too far away? There is none visible on the road ahead, but wait a minute! Wasn't there a gas station about half way up that last hill? Surely there was—on the right-hand side of the road, with two gas pumps, and only about a quarter of a mile away.

Now at last you have it. The problem has been diagnosed. The solution has been found. The only thing that remains is to put this likely solution to the actual test. And so you walk back down the road, find the station open, buy a gallon of gas in a borrowed can, return to your car, start the engine, and the thought-process is over—until the next time.

All real thinking follows this same general pattern. Let us see how it works out in thinking through the very difficult problem of Negro-white relationships in our nation.

The first step is to diagnose the problem. What is the nub of the difficulty? Is it overpopulation, too many people trying to live in a limited area, and getting into one another's way until tension results? Hardly! Even though the number of Americans has been growing rapidly, there is still elbow-room in America. Is it the threat and the fear of intermarriage between the races? In the eyes of many white people this is a real sore-spot, but to Negroes scarcely at all. They do not particularly desire intermarriage, and are not greatly concerned about it. Could the root of the trouble be economic? Perhaps so! We recall that the lynching rate goes up as the price of cotton goes down, and vice versa. Negroes, who are greatly underprivileged, are anxious to get more of this world's goods than they have thus far had. And whites are anxious to keep what they have. The result is rivalry, tension, mistrust, bitterness. For the time being at least, we settle on this as a major part of the problem to be solved.

The next step is to cast about for solutions of this problem. What is to be done about it? Would better education for both Negroes and white people help at all, enabling our citizenry all along the line to fit better into the productive processes of our nation? Would there be any gain in trying to expand the number of bi-racial labor unions, so that the two races might have more opportunity to work things out together? Or should the approach be by way of rehabilitating thousands of acres of land in the South, on which countless people now eke out a slim existence? Or does the solution lie rather in the direction of more bi-racial churches? Among these various solutions, and others which might be included, which is soundest economically? Which is closest to the spirit of Jesus?

The third step—which really goes a bit beyond the thought-process itself—is to try out one or more solutions of the problem in actual practice, and then perhaps revise the strategy, or even start all over again, in the light of the experience gained.

Greatly simplified, this is real thinking. It can be applied to the choice of a vocation, the construction of a budget for one's personal use, the building of a program for a youth fellowship, the problem of boy-girl relationships, the control of atomic power, or any other puzzling issue large or small in the life of the individual or of society. It can be done by a solitary individual or by a number of people in cooperation, in which case it is called group thinking or group discussion. As far as we know, human beings are the only creatures that can really think. It is, therefore, one of our unique and priceless privileges. We ought to do a great deal of it, probably much more than we ordinarily do. It is one of the best ways to climb the ladder from earth to heaven.

Who Made the Ladder?

Forming habits, shaping attitudes, thinking things through— none of these is a mere hit or miss affair. All of them proceed according to definite laws and principles. Who made these laws and principles? All of them, if done well and constructively, represent a steady climb on the ladder of growth. Who set up this ladder?

Clearly we didn't. These processes were going on, and going on just this way, long before we were born. Cromagnon men in the caves of France thousands of years ago formed habits then just as we do today. The ancient Israelites developed attitudes toward the Philistines and the Assyrians in the same way as we develop attitudes toward the Japanese or the Russians. The old Greeks followed exactly the same process of thought as the one we follow, and did very well indeed!

It is equally clear that the psychologists didn't set it up. They have discovered these various laws and principles and processes, but they didn't make them. They simply studied minutely and formulated clearly what was already there. Some psychological

44

laws do indeed bear the name of a man, as, for example, Thorndike's Laws of Learning; but this means only that the man in question reduced them to clear form. He did not create them.

Who then did? God did. He ordained the laws and principles, and wrote them into the structure of things for our own good. He set up the ladder of growth. If we climb it patiently, round by round, it will lead us to him.

Lord, all my desire is before thee.

—PSALM 38: 9

4

DESIRES AND DODGES

Our conduct is often determined by motives of which we are quite unaware. People who fondly imagine that they are actuated by nothing but a sense of duty are often surprised to discover that the real motive of their conduct is the gratification of some latent desire. The politician, of course, desires only to serve his country, the clergyman to preach the truth, the ascetic to practice self-denial, the doctor seeks only the health of his patients, the researcher the interests of science, the slum worker to uplift the masses, and the saint seeks holiness. These are the conscious motives. When analysed, it may be found that the original motives which led them to these lines of action were—in the politician, self-importance; the clergyman, self-display; the ascetic, a shrinking from the responsibilities of life; the doctor, his reputation; the scientist, curiosity; the saint, self-righteousness; the slum-worker, a social snobbishness, which urges him to seek the society of people amongst whom he will be "somebody."

—From *Psychology and Morals*, by J. A. HADFIELD. Medill McBride and Company. Used by permission.

THE NOTION is frequently held that we are primarily thinking-machines, but such a picture of human nature is quite misleading. As a matter of fact, it is much closer to the truth to say that we are primarily bundles of wants and wishes. Thinking is, of course, most important. It plays the same role in life as a coachman driving a team of spirited horses. Without a driver, the coach would swerve blindly in any direction, probably get off the road sooner or later, and possibly end in a tangled wreck. But without the horses, the coach would not move at all. In the same way, it is our basic desires that make the wheels go round.

Perhaps the two questions most essential to self-understanding are, What do we want in life? and, What happens when we don't get it?

What Do We Want in Life?

As we observe people, we see them doing all sorts of strange things. Here is a boy taking severe bumps and bruises in football practice, and doing without chocolate sundaes for weeks at a time. Why does he do it? Almost equally puzzling is the spectacle of a girl painstakingly touching up her natural face with various concoctions of powder and paint. Why does she go to so much trouble? Or consider a group of students hanging breathlessly over an interesting laboratory experiment to see what will happen. Why should they care what will happen? Stranger still is the case of a mother slaving endlessly for a baby who won't be able to do anything for her in many years. Why should she "put herself out" in such unaccountable fashion for a helpless infant? Perhaps strangest of all is a Trappist monk withdrawing from the world of affairs and living for fifty years in seclusion and silence. What deep desires impel him to spend his life in this manner?

Almost every psychologist has his own formulation of the basic desires of human nature, the inner mainspring which makes us tick. One of the most useful and widely accepted is the list of Four Wishes made by a sociologist named W. I. Thomas. As we run over it, point by point, ask yourself how well it accounts for all the various things we do and the many interests and ambitions we cherish. According to this student, what we want in life mainly is the following:

1. *Recognition.* We want to be widely recognized for what we are and for what we can do. We want to "be somebody." We want to stand well in the eyes of others—a class, a school, a youth fellowship, a gang, the community as a whole. Under

47

this heading falls a large part of our close attention to the number of dates we have; the number of offices we hold; the grades we get on our report cards; the length of our personal sketches in the school annual; the clothes we wear; the money we carry in our pockets; not to mention various and sundry items such as the ability to dance well, and to converse on the latest topic in the latest slang. In all of these respects, and many others which could be mentioned, we want to hold our own with everyone else, and be a little out in front if possible.

Why should we be so anxious to be well thought of by others? Their opinions of us don't make us a bit better, or a bit worse. As Pop-eye so eloquently put it: "I yam what I yam, and that's all I yam." Nevertheless, the fact remains that this is one of the strongest desires of life. The savage is just as anxious to have a long string of lions' teeth around his neck and a large number of wives in his harem as we are to have a long convertible and a large selection of dates—and pretty much for the same reason. The little child wants a pile of blocks that will give him prestige in the kindergarten, and the aged man wants a tombstone that will compare favorably with any other in the cemetery. Sometimes this wish becomes stronger than the will-to-live itself. A soldier may prefer the chance of death to the charge of cowardice. And so, from the cradle to the grave, each of us strives for his own place in the sun.

2. *Response.* We want the friendly, affectionate response of others to us. We want to be cared for. We want to be liked by parents, brother and sister, boy friend and girl friend. This is somewhat different from the wish for recognition. It is not enough to be recognized by fifty or five hundred. We are hungry also to be loved and befriended by three or four, or half a dozen—not because we are brilliant, capable, or good-looking, but just because we are ourselves.

This also is a strong and compelling force in our lives. It accounts for a good many of our feelings and actions: the time and energy we spend on making and keeping friends; our desire to have dates (in part at least); and our deep attachment to our families. In fact, this is a major part of the cement which holds friendships, love affairs, cliques, and families together. Without it, life would be much poorer, and much less interesting.

3. *Security*. We want to be safe. We want to be sure of ourselves (here we are quite close to the wish for recognition). We want to be sure of our place in the affection of our family and our friends (here we are close to response). We want to be able to see our way through the difficulties that surround us today, or may befall us tomorrow. We are so little, and life is so big; we have a tremendous desire to be secure.

This wish crops out in a number of different ways. This is why a little child runs to his parents, climbs in their laps, and watches anxiously every word and action on their part. He is trying to reassure himself that he is secure with them. This is why, in part at least, we study to fit ourselves for a vocation. We want to make our own futures secure. This is why we buy life insurance, health insurance, fire insurance, accident insurance. We are trying to safeguard ourselves against anything that may upset our security. This is why, not only in Christianity but also in some other religions, the doctrine of salvation looms so large. For "salvation" comes from a Latin word which means "safe." We want to be sure that we are safe—not only with men but also with God, not only in this life but also in eternity.

4. *New experience*. We want to "go places and see things." We want to taste something new, learn something new, do something new, try something new, see something new. We are never quite satisfied to remain where we are. There is always something beyond toward which we reach out. This has often been called a "divine discontent." It is discontent, all right; and there seems to be something divine about it. As far as we know, only human beings experience it. A contented cow doesn't know what it means, but we do. Perhaps this is a part of God's image upon us. He has made us restless with what we are and eager for something more.

49

Here is much of the explanation of our studying, our reading, our traveling, our buying of new things, our changing from one job to another, our moving from one place to another, our shifting from one interest to another. As long as we are truly alive, we never stand still. We are ever in motion.

To this list of four wishes must be added, of course, such body-drives as hunger and sex. We then have—do we not?—a pretty good working description of the fundamental desires of mankind. Is there something that should be added? Can you think of anything we do which cannot be traced to one or another of these sources?

What Happens When We Don't Get It?

Often life doesn't give us everything we want. This may be good, or it may be bad; but it is undeniably true. Take, for instance, the imaginary example of a high school boy who has been a victim of infantile paralysis. Within him are all four of the wishes described in the previous section, but his crippled leg and the way life is set up get in his way. He would like the recognition of his associates, but he can't play football and even tennis is a severe strain upon him. He would like to win the intimate response of others, but dancing goes hard with him and the most attractive girls are likely to be otherwise engaged when he calls up for a date. He would like to make his future secure, but many vocations are closed to him. He would like to go places and see things with the rest of the crowd, but he can't get around so well as the others and many interesting experiences are denied him. And so a conflict arises between what he wants and what he actually gets.

It is not at all serious if this conflict remains out in the open, where he can see it and talk about it and laugh at it a little. No particular harm is done by our becoming thirsty for a Coke, and not being able to drink one. We are not getting what we want, but nobody suffers a nervous breakdown from having to do without a Coke.

50

However, sometimes our wants and feelings are shoved down below the level of consciousness—and that is a different matter entirely! Psychologists tell us that the experiences we remember and the feelings of which we are aware make up only a fraction of ourselves. We are like icebergs, with perhaps one-tenth above water level and the other nine-tenths below. Down there below "water level" lie many things, including some we don't want to remember and are ashamed to admit. This is called the unconscious. Now if our imaginary student has made several attempts at dancing which have brought him only deep humiliation, he may without knowing it thrust these memories and even the wish to be a good dancer and popular with the girls down below the level of consciousness. This doesn't wipe out the basic desires; it merely submerges them. They are still there. And they may come out in all sorts of strange ways, which are as mysterious to the boy as to everyone else. This is conflict of a more serious nature.

We are now ready to look at some of the peculiar dodges we resort to when we don't get what we want. Each person, of course, finds his own way out of such a difficulty. But there is a bag of standard tricks which a person is rather likely to employ. We cannot survey them all, but only several of the more common and more important ones. When we don't get what we want, what then?

1. *We pretend we didn't want it anyhow.* This is called the "sour grapes" dodge, so named from the fable of the fox who tried to reach a bunch of grapes above his head and concluded they must be sour and undesirable when he found he couldn't get them. The boy whom we are using as an illustration may have wanted with all his heart to be football captain. But when he realizes this is impossible, he can give you seventeen sound reasons why nobody in his right mind would want to be captain of a football team. He is merely trying to fool himself and everyone else by labeling "sour" that which he can't get.

The opposite of this is the "sweet lemon" dodge. The "lemon"

51

that we have to take, whether we like it or not, is called "sweet" to make it as palatable as possible.

Closely related to these is "rationalization," which means simply trying to find good and plausible reasons for doing what we were going to do anyhow. In true thinking, the reasoning process comes at the beginning, and guides the decision that is made. In rationalization, the decision is made first on some other basis, and then so-called reasoning is beckoned in to make the whole thing look respectable. For example, a dance may be in the offing. The truth is that we want to go to the dance. But we may feel that we have to dress the matter up a little to ease our own consciences or to "get by" with our parents. And so we begin to talk about the good this would do our health, or the beauty of the music produced by this particular dance band, or even the help we might give a class-mate who is coming to the dance and will need someone to show him around. This is rationalization.

2. *We substitute something else "just as good."* Our student, upon giving up athletics, may develop a sudden passion for modern drama, or classical music, or he may even take to continuous wisecracking in order to gain the attention he so desperately wants. The fact that this is not what he actually wanted is given away by his overdone enthusiasm for the new interest. He will buttonhole you every time he meets you in the hall, and talk about nothing but modern drama. Or he will play records of classical music by the hour. Or he will carry his attempts at wisecracking to pitiful lengths. What he is try-ing to do is to convince himself, as well as you, that this is what he really wanted all along; whereas, of course, it wasn't at all.

3. *We take it out in daydreaming.* The would-be football hero may picture himself tucking the ball serenely under his arm, and weaving nonchalantly through the opposing team for a ninety-yard run while the stands go wild. In a daydream it is ninety yards or nothing—never a modest, hard-won three-yard

gain. This is one of the chief marks of these imaginary exploits: they are generally extravagant. After all, there is no point in daydreaming a mere three-yard push through the line. Another mark is a convenient by-passing of all the hard work required in real life to accomplish something fine. In actual football, a ninety-yard run comes only after months of grueling practice and daily self-denial. But in the daydream, a person sits comfortably in his chair and whisks himself with the greatest of ease into heroism.

In both these respects, daydreaming is quite different from real life, and altogether different from hard and cold realistic planning for the future. For example, it is one thing for a person to picture himself as a doctor ten years from now, seeing the life of a doctor as it actually is, and planning sensibly for all the intermediate steps between here and there. It is quite another thing to leap at once into the joys of being hailed as a world-famous surgeon. The former is wholesome planning, about which the individual intends to do something. The latter is unwholesome fantasy, about which the individual intends to do nothing at all. It is too easy. It is unreal. It may become a dangerous substitute for the real thing.

4. *We blame our failure on someone else.* To return to our example, this boy may rail against the football coach, and everyone else. The coach is prejudiced. The teachers play favorites. The students are cliquish. The failure is really in himself, but it is so much easier to attach the blame to someone else! This is called "projection," which means a "hurling forward." The fault is lifted up from oneself, and hurled forward until it lands on someone "out there" in the world beyond.

Individuals do this time and again, and so do whole peoples. After World War I, the Germans could not stand to think that they themselves had failed; so they fastened the blame on the Jews, making them the scapegoats. Much racial prejudice, the psychologists say, comes about through just this sort of scapegoating.

To come back to the individual, occasionally a person will go so far with this dodge that he pictures the whole world as being against him. A giant conspiracy may be conjured up, with the War Department, the Pope, and the Masons all combining to do him harm. This is called "paranoia," which means literally that a person is "out of his mind." And so he is, for such a person has got so far away from things as they actually are that he is no longer sane.

5. *We cover up by blustering.* Under the circumstances we have pictured, our student may begin to act big and bold, perhaps swearing a little and throwing his weight around right and left. It is not hard to see what he is doing. He is covering up his weakness and his failure by overstressing the exact opposite of weakness and failure. He is trying hard, too hard, to prove to himself and others that he is big and strong and successful.

This is called "over-compensation"—an overdone attempt on the surface to make up for a dimly sensed weakness farther down in the person's life. Here belongs the much discussed inferiority complex. Its true representative is not poor Caspar Milquetoast, afraid to call his soul his own. He doesn't have an inferiority complex; he is just inferior. No, the shining example of this dodge is rather the loud, argumentative fellow who shouts and fights at the least provocation. You see, he is busy all the time trying to prove to himself that he is really a man—which only goes to show how unsure he is of himself.

Over-compensation comes out in other forms also. A person who knows that liquor is his weakness may make long and ardent speeches against intemperance. He is trying valiantly to make up on the surface for a dimly sensed weakness farther down in his life. He is squaring accounts with his own conscience, or trying to do so. He is attempting to hide his weakness from himself and from others. A mother who resents having a stepchild to care for may try to cover up to herself and the child by an over-display of false affection.

6. *We go to the movies, or read books.* The student in question, denied on every hand what he wants and needs so badly, may drift off to the movies. There he can see a brave, bold, handsome, hard-shooting, lady-killing son of the west, whose exploits embody everything he would like to be but isn't. For a little while he can identify himself with his screen hero (hence this dodge is called "identification"), and share in all the glory of this other self. Men fear him. Women love him. When he comes out of the theater, he may even swagger a little as he walks down the pavement of his home town. He is really not himself. For the time being, he is "this other." Or, lacking the money to go to the movies, he may settle down with a cheap book and get the same results at a lower price without leaving the comfort of his favorite chair.

Not all movie attendance and not all book reading belong in this class by any means. But it is safe to say both the theater owners and the book sellers would be a good deal poorer, if it were not for this tendency to seek a secondhand thrill by identifying ourselves with the dashing men and the glamorous women on the silver screen and the printed page. What, you may say, is wrong with it? The same thing that is wrong with daydreaming. It is too easy. It is unreal. It may become a cheap substitute for the real thing.

7. *We fall back on overeating, oversmoking, and overdrinking.* Many a woman, whose husband or neighbors don't treat her as she thinks they ought, reaches for a handy box of chocolates. Many a man, who doesn't get what he wants in life, seeks relief from his nervousness and sense of frustration by chain-smoking. And many people find in alcohol a way out of their difficulties. In fact, excessive and chronic drinking is perhaps best thought of in numerous cases as an escape from the bitter realities of life with chemical assistance. As a poor, beaten-down man in the slums of Chicago said, "It is the quickest way to get away from the stockyards." Experimenters have turned even cats to drink by worrying the soul out of

them. This is not to justify alcoholism. It is merely to say that many heavy drinkers will not be cured until they find some better way of getting what they really want in life.

These are some of the most common and important dodges. There are others, including a few that can be quite serious. But these are the ordinary, garden-variety dodges. Have you ever seen them used by anyone you know? Have you ever used any of them yourself?

Can We Be Happy Anyhow?

If life denies us some of the things we want, can we be happy nevertheless? Of course we can—on one condition, namely, that we are honest with ourselves. To refer once more to our imaginary high school student, he can find much happiness in life provided he admits to himself fully and frankly that he would really have liked to be football captain. There is still much left. There are books, music, friendships, sunsets, work, and faith in God. What more can one want?

Many people live out a part of their lives on second bests, and it is a good way to live, provided there is no attempt to disguise the truth. All deception is bad, but self-deception is worst of all. Life is like a hotel corridor, from which a number of rooms open out. A person may try a certain door, and find the door tightly locked. There are other doors and other rooms, as worth entering as the first one. Let him go in elsewhere, and live happily with no regrets. Only, if he really wanted the first door, he will do well to say: "That is where I would have preferred to go. But I could not. Therefore, I will enter here, and be grateful for everything I find." This is the way to mental health and happiness.

Jesus gave his disciples the assurance, "You will know the truth, and the truth will make you free." Nowhere is this clearer and surer than in our own individual lives. The more we face the truth, the freer we become. We may of course have to lean on some trusted counselor for a while, if life has been hard on us and the truth is none too pleasant. But we no longer have to pretend. We need not resort to any dodges. We are free to move forward, getting along without the things life denies us, and enjoying to the full the many blessings it affords.

Are We Never Unselfish?

All of this chapter thus far appears to be looking out for Number One. Are we always selfish? Yes, to begin with. A little child doesn't care the least bit about anyone but himself. If he wants a drink in the middle of the night, his style isn't cramped in the least by the thought that perhaps his mother is dead tired from washing the day before and his father has to get up early the next morning to go to work. He is concerned about himself alone. But as he gets older, several things happen in succession.

First, he finds that he has to think of others somewhat in order to be happy himself. He can't take his brother's toys at will, for his brother will come down on him hard and he himself will become unpopular—and he doesn't want that. He can't drag dirt into the kitchen or turn the radio up to a boom while his father is reading the evening paper, for mother and father will think less of him—and he doesn't want that. This is the first long step toward a regard for others.

Next, he begins to "feel with" others when they are happy: his brother enjoying his own toys, his mother taking satisfaction in a clean kitchen, and his father brightening up during a well deserved rest. He can understand how they feel, for he has been in like situations himself. And so he feels with them. This is the second step.

Finally, this happiness in seeing and making others happy grows. Such happiness has one great advantage—it doesn't lead to self-consciousness. The more a person concentrates on himself, the more he becomes aware of himself, and the unhappier he is. Pure self-seeking is thus self-defeating. It doesn't get anywhere. A person can't practice it forever with satisfaction. But,

57

on the contrary, the joy that comes from seeing a glow on someone else's face is not tainted and spoiled by self-consciousness. It can keep right on growing. A person can practice it forever with increasing satisfaction. The laws of growth, therefore, in the long run are weighted on the side of a regard for others. And in the end this child can reach the point where it does him more good to see his brother get a bicycle than to have one himself.

It seems, therefore, that God has so made us that we win our way to a regard for others with great difficulty, but we are never fully happy until we get there. He might have created us to become unselfish automatically, but that would have been too easy. At the other extreme, he might have made us and life without this constant restless pull toward others. Then we would never have reached unselfishness. Instead, he did things just right. Truly his ways with men are wonderful, and wonderfully good.

For I was my father's son, tender and only beloved in the sight of my mother.

5

THOSE APRON STRINGS

Some people look upon parent and child as of necessity being completely absorbed in each other. That is to say, a parent does not live for anything but that which ministers to the child and the child responds by living a life that is completely wrapped up in the parent. As one citizen wrote to his Congressman, in an attempt to have his runaway son sent home from the army, "I raised this boy for my own use." Important as the rearing of children is, in the long run this sort of relationship does not prove to be the best. It leads to the stifling of individuality rather than to freeing it. It leads to slavery of one to the other instead of gradually achieved freedom.

—From *The Home and Christian Living,* by PERCY R. and MYRTLE H. HAYWARD. Westminster Press. Copyright 1931. Used by permission.

A FEW YEARS ago a visitor to the campus of one of our institutions of higher learning might have witnessed the strange sight of a mother and her son going everywhere side by side. The boy, as it happened, was a near-genius. He finished college by the time he was fifteen, and received his doctor's degree at the age of nineteen or thereabouts. Everywhere he went, his mother went along—to classroom, library, or dining-hall. One could almost see the apron strings binding the two together.

While this is an extreme case, in every normal person's life those apron strings are present. They constitute one of the most important facts of life. And the way they are handled has a great deal to do with personality-growth throughout childhood and adolescence.

What Makes Them So Strong?

This question virtually answers itself. The oldest and firmest ties linking us with other persons are those between us and our parents, especially our mothers. During the very years when personality is taking its distinctive shape, the infant lives and moves and has his being in his home. At first he never leaves the house except in the company of his parents, and even later he scarcely ever goes beyond the yard. Father and mother are his constant companions. To them he looks for everything he needs—food, shelter, toys, medical care, comfort, encouragement, affection, security. Without them, he is nothing; indeed he could not live at all. In particular, he is thrown into almost hourly contact with his mother. Father may be away at work during most of the hours he is awake. But mother is always there, a very present help in time of trouble.

Under such circumstances, ties of unusual strength are slowly but surely woven between the young child and his parents. They are everything to him. They can do no wrong. They are the source of all good. And the child is everything to his parents. Their lives revolve around him. They work for him, plan for him, watch over him when he is sick, note proudly his first tooth and his first step across the room—and hurry over to the neighbors to tell them about it. So closely knit are these bonds of mutual love and dependence that in later years they are hard to loosen.

On the child's side, he experiences great difficulty in changing his feelings toward his parents. He has cherished this loving dependence upon them so long that it has become a habit, one of the fundamental habits of his life. To alter it in any degree is almost as hard as to shift from writing with one hand to writing with the other. An old book in a Sunday school library told of a young man who played the violin quite well, but made his living as a clerk in a butcher shop. One day he saw a heavy cleaver about to fall on a child's arm, and reached out his left hand to check the blow. He saved the child, but severed the tendons in his hand so that he could no longer finger the violin. So he set about the task of learning all over again, fingering with his good right hand and bowing with the stiffened fingers of his left. Something like that is involved in changing a child's emotional bent toward his parents. Or, take another example that perhaps each of us can appreciate. Imagine that you have come up through school under a certain teacher, and twenty years later find yourself on the same faculty with your old instructor. You may call all your other colleagues by their first names, but not this man! The old relationship runs too deep. Once your teacher, always your teacher. In the same way, once your parent, always your parent.

Furthermore, in many respects the child gets quite a bit of satisfaction out of the old dependent relationship, even when he is no longer a child in years. It is very nice to be mothered and fathered. It is quite pleasant at ten, or twenty, or thirty to have someone to ease the nasty bumps, and make the hard decisions. Such solid joys are not lightly laid aside. And so the apron strings remain.

On the parents' side, they too find it difficult to change their feelings. When they first made their child's acquaintance, he was a helpless baby. Now that he is ten or twenty, his body has grown mightily but he is still the same to them. Whenever they look at him, even though they have to look up, they tend to see the little baby they first knew. Surely he is not big enough to go to a city a hundred miles away alone! Or drive an automobile! Or decide all by himself what vocation he is going to follow! Why, it just seems like yesterday that he was lying in the crib there by the window, kicking his heels into the air. This isn't wickedness or stubbornness on the part of parents. It is just habit, an old reliable habit of very long

61

standing which is colored by some of the deepest emotions of which we are capable.

Besides, there is real satisfaction to the parents in keeping their child dependent on them. How nice it is to have someone come running to you for a few kind words when he is in trouble, or a bit of advice when he is in difficulty! You are still needed. You have not lost your importance. Of course, a parent rarely admits to himself how much he is enjoying this relationship. That wouldn't do at all. No, he pictures himself as thinking purely and simply of the child, and the child's own good. Just trying to be a good mother or father—that is all! But in reality the parent is getting quite a boost to his own self-esteem. In the case of the mother, we may go a step farther and say that her children are her job, her vocation, her life-work. They are to her what a business or profession is to the father. In them she invests her life. By their success she is judged. And when they leave home, she is literally out of a job. She goes through an experience similar to the father's when he retires. It is all over. Her usefulness is ended. Naturally, she fights against this day, and postpones it as long as possible. And thus the apron strings cling on.

In certain situations, the ties are knit unusually tight. It is well to know what these are, and to be on the lookout for them.

First, an isolated rural home. In the country parents and children are thrown into closer and more constant contact with each other than in the city. There isn't anyone else. They work together, play together, live together. Father and mother are home all day, and almost every evening. So are brother and sister, except for school. There are no gangs, clubs, or movies nearby. The family roof shelters them all, and there is little opportunity for getting away from it. As a consequence, rural youth have probably grown up a bit more shy, more hesitant about making new contacts, and more dependent upon their parents than city youth. However, it should be quickly added that this situation is changing rapidly. The automobile and the

62

radio, but chiefly the automobile, are wiping out the distinctions between town and country. Before long, it may be impossible to tell the difference.

Second, an only child. If there are ten children in a family, the parents may love them all with all their hearts, but there just isn't time enough to hover over any one of them, or money enough to squander much on any of them. They have to shift for themselves a good bit. But in the case of an only child, all the affection and all the possessions of the family gravitate toward him alone, and he may get an overdose of both. Besides, he has no one else near his own age in the family, and associates largely with people twenty or thirty years older than he is. As a result, he may (not necessarily must) grow up unhealthily close to his parents.

Third, the youngest child. An older brother or sister goes through something which "the baby" of the family never has to face, namely, the experience of being displaced from the center of attention by a new and very cute and helpless arrival. He has no successor. Often, though not always by any means, he continues to be petted and babied much too long for his own good. This tendency is most marked where a fair-haired little girl comes along in the wake of three or four boys; or one chubby boy after three or four girls.

Fourth, a sickly child. In the nature of the case, father and mother—especially mother—must give such a child an unusual amount of attention. He must be specially fed, clothed, and cared for. He is shielded against bumps, bruises, drafts, rough games, and rough playmates. Sometimes, though not invariably, this protection is carried much too far, and continued too long.

Fifth, the death of one parent. This leaves the other parent lonely and hungry for affection. The most logical persons to satisfy such hunger are the children. Thus, if a father dies, the mother may lean heavily toward and upon her son. And, if a mother dies, the father may turn the full force of his affection upon his daughter. On the other hand, sometimes the death of a parent compels children to depend upon themselves more, and grow up faster than would otherwise be the case.

Sixth, a lack of complete understanding and affection between the parents. In such a case, either or both of the parents may turn toward the children to make up for what they should have but do not find with each other. This is hard on the children. At a time when they should be young and carefree, they are called upon to pinch-hit emotionally for a husband or a wife.

Is it any wonder that the apron strings become strong?

Some Keep Them Too Long

When these family ties between the generations are knit too tight and kept too long, everybody suffers. It is hard to say which suffer the more, but probably the younger generation.

The teen-ager who finds himself bound hand and foot by apron strings is not able to get along well with others of his own age. He is not at ease with them. To tell the truth, he is not a full person, but a puppet bobbing along at the end of apron strings. He is not free to be himself. His mind must turn back constantly and unnaturally to mother and father, and what they would think. So the boy shows up at a football game wearing the rubbers which his mother put on, and the girl is uncomfortable at a party because father has a headache and may be needing her this very minute. Since they are so ill at ease with their own kind and age, such boys and girls often attach themselves to older people, whom they understand better. They hang around the classroom a little too much to talk with the teacher. They are a little too anxious to consult the minister on deep problems. They develop a crush on a club leader. What they are doing is easy enough to understand. They are carrying on outside the home the same pattern which their home life laid deep in their natures.

An adolescent who is overly dependent upon his parents is not able to stand fully on his own feet in any matter. He can't make his own decisions, but must wait for his parents—or someone like his parents—to make them for him. He can't take the initiative in anything, but must hold back until someone else goes ahead as his parents have always done. He can't even work out his own religious beliefs, but must simply take over unthinkingly the faith of his parents. In extreme cases this utter dependence upon another can become pitiful indeed. A young man with a splendid mind but a timid spirit went through college and medical school and hung out his shingle in a small town as a doctor. Two or three weeks later, after a promising start, he suddenly closed his office and went back to mother. Whatever reasons he may have given to himself or the community, the truth of the matter was that he simply couldn't face life on his own. There were too many people to be met; too many diagnoses to be made; too many difficulties to be faced. Although he was twenty-five years old and fully trained, he was not grown up emotionally. At heart he was still his mother's little boy, not ready as yet for a man's responsibilities.

Apron strings can also hold a young person back from happy marriage. For the son who is too close to his mother is really not free to love another woman. And the daughter who dotes on her father is not free to turn her affections fully toward another man. How many marriages have been prevented by apron strings, and how much unhappiness has been caused within marriages, no one will ever know. Unfortunately for the male sex, the sons are harder hit in this respect than the daughters. For it is the mother, not the father, who stays at home, nurses the children, spends time with them, and weaves strands of affection between herself and them. Hence, there are more mama's boys than there are daddy's girls, and more men than women are held back from successful marriage by these home ties. For this reason, as well as some others, there is more mother-in-law trouble than father-in-law trouble. You have heard many mother-in-law jokes. How many do you know about a father-in-law? But it is not a joking matter, none of it.

Instead it brings heartaches to husbands and wives, and condemns some children in the next generation to the fate of growing up in a tense and unhappy home. And thus the unfortunate consequences go on and on.

Yet another result is that the overdependent youth may look throughout his life for someone to mother or father him (or her). He is so used to it that he can't get along without it. So everyone with whom he is thrown into close contact is a candidate—teacher, doctor, pastor, husband or wife, "Y" secretary, or employer. He expects them to treat him as mother and father did, and is disappointed or offended if they do not. They must show him special consideration as though he were a favored child, and shoulder the burdens which he is not mature enough to carry himself.

Finally, our list of consequences would be incomplete if we did not note that every now and then a young person rebels strongly against such overprotection, and strikes out on his own. Perhaps he is simply tired of having a conducted tour through life. Or it may be that he is ashamed of his dependence. At any rate, if and when he rebels, he often goes to extremes. Away with everything his home has stood for! He may quit going to church, just because his parents go. Or he may start attending church with great regularity, just because his parents do not. If his parents are musicians, he decides to go into business—merely to be different! Everything they stand for is discarded, and everything they suggest is rejected. This too is pathetic. In the fervent desire for independence, which is everybody's right in due time, he has cast aside not only the bad in his relationships with his parents but the good also. He has to do so, you see, in order to make sure he has the freedom he wants. But what a heavy price both he and the parents pay!

To turn briefly to the effects upon the older generation, they suffer too when the apron strings are drawn too tight and kept too long. If the child kicks over the traces in obvious rebellion, they are hurt. If he or she fails to make a go of life and remains merely a grown up infant, they are hurt—even though they themselves were unintentionally to blame. But this is not all! Parents who have lived in and for their children to an unwise degree are left high and dry when they finally leave home. There seems to be so little left to live for. Sometimes an attempt is made to keep the same close hold on mature sons and daughters when they are fat and forty. But this close watchfulness over daily comings and goings is quite naturally resented. And so the unhappiness spreads back and forth.

In the scheme of life, each new person should start out within the loving care of a good home, grow by easy stages into the freedom of manhood and womanhood, surround the next generation with the care it needs, set it free in turn, and so on to the end of time. Whenever this scheme is tampered with, the result is trouble for all concerned.

Some Break Them Too Soon

Thus far our consideration of apron strings may have left the impression that harm can follow only from keeping them tied too long. But there is also the danger of casting them off too soon. Only now a different sort of harm results.

Instead of a teen-ager who is not comfortable with others of his own age, we get one who is too comfortable. He is with them all the time. The gang takes the place of the home, and his parents' counsel doesn't hold a candle to what the crowd says and does.

Instead of an adolescent who can't stand on his own feet, we have one who won't stand anywhere else, even when they are a little shaky. He insists on making his own decisions in both big and small matters. And it is just as far from the truth for a sixteen-year-old to think he knows all the answers as to fear that he doesn't know any of them.

Instead of a young person who is not free to love anyone of the opposite sex truly, we see a Romeo who can love them all a little, and does so.

Instead of a dependent looking wistfully on every street corner for someone to serve as a mother or father, we find the very essence of independence—not taking anything from anybody.

Instead of parents who have hovered over their children too long, we are dealing with the opposite type who haven't stayed sufficiently close to their children to bless them with the fruits of their own rich experience.

In modern life a number of circumstances combine to point life in this direction for some families. Many a father nowadays, against his will, is an absentee parent. If his work does not take him away from home for a week or so at a time, he may be a commuter. From his suburban home he has an hour's ride to his work in the city each morning, and an hour's return trip each evening. This makes a long day, and father doesn't count too much in the life of the home. In a suburban area opposite New York City, the delinquency rate took a turn downward during the depression of the 1930's. Men who would have been away from home all day were now out of work, so that children had their fathers for a while. Unemployment may have cut down their allowances, but it was good for their souls. It returned their fathers to them.

As for mother, she too may work in factory and office nowadays. During World War II the number of women employed in industry increased tremendously. When the fighting ended, many of them gave up their jobs, but not all of them. Some had to continue for the sake of the family's finances, and others simply enjoyed the freedom and extra money. In either case, the children were left without either father or mother during most of the daylight hours. If mother does not work outside the home, the modern labor-saving devices have simplified her housekeeping duties so that she has more time for bridge clubs and community activities. So she is often away a good deal, and interested in other things. All this makes for an added measure of independence on the part of the children.

68

Besides, city life itself tends to weaken the hold of the home on boys and girls. The home no longer has a monopoly on their lives. There are so many other places for them to be, and so many other standards for them to follow. All day long they are in school. When they return home, they may throw their books in the front door and dash out again to play in the streets. After supper there are the movies, clubs, the "Y," a teen-age center, or simply more roaming the streets again. Whether these activities are good or bad, they are at least outside the family. Home becomes for some a place to eat, sleep, and hang up one's hat—and that is about all. In addition, the modern trend in education teaches children and young people to think for themselves. This is equally true of school, church, and club. It is the spirit of the times. No one would wish it otherwise, except when it goes too far. Then it turns out boys and girls who are prematurely independent. Instead of maturing too slowly, they grow up too fast for their own good.

The net result of all these factors is a certain number of homes where the apron strings are too weak, and are broken too soon. The parents have abdicated. The children are hard, self-willed, defiant, and sometimes delinquent. The outcome is heartache for both.

The Art of Untying Them

It begins to look as though these apron strings must be handled just right. On the one hand, they serve a real purpose. We could not get along without them. On the other hand, they can strangle and smother life. So they must be gradually untied. This is one of the finest of the fine arts, requiring skill on the part of parents and children alike.

From infancy on, each child should spend some time with his parents and some time with others of his own age. The best solution is probably a gradual transition from the one to the other. The important word here is "gradual." To begin with, it may be ninety-five per cent with parents, and five per cent

69

with his fellows; then eighty and twenty; then sixty and forty; and finally, when he is grown, perhaps five and ninety-five. If he moves too fast, the parents can hold him back and find interesting things for them all to do together. If he moves too slowly, they can push him tenderly out of the nest and encourage him to go on his own.

From infancy on, a child should increasingly make his own decisions. At first none at all. Then such a matter as whether or not to eat his potatoes, or whether to have two desserts or only one. Then how to spend a nickel or a dime. Then the choice of the clothes he will wear to school. Then whether to play baseball on a nice spring evening or to study. And finally such crucial decisions as the selection of a vocation, or a husband or wife. The picture is that of a rectangle, with a diagonal running from the upper left-hand corner to the lower right-hand. The bottom triangle is the parents' direction of the life of their child. The top triangle is his own growing self-reliance. As the one declines, the other increases—step by step, little by little.

From the time their children are born, parents do well to cultivate some interests apart from their children. At first, of course, a little baby may need all the care and affection they can lavish upon him. That is right and proper. As the years of childhood come and go, the need continues, but in diminishing degree. Without resigning as parents, they should sooner or later begin to find something outside their children to live for. This may sound heartless, but it is necessary both for their own sakes and for their children's sakes. They do not stop loving the boys and girls whom they have brought into the world; that will never happen. They merely avoid being absorbed in them alone. Perhaps father and mother will go to a movie together, as they did in their courting days. Or they will locate some hobbies which they can pursue as a couple or as individuals. In this way the children can gradually move into the freedom they need. They are not the sole support of their parents. And the "old folks at home" will have something to live for when the sons and daughters are grown and established in homes of their own.

And what is the eventual outcome of this slow and artful untying of the apron strings? We must be very clear at this point, lest wrong impressions be created. It is not that parents and children become cold toward each other; not at all. Father and mother still regard their children with true warmth of affection, but as grown men and women—not helpless infants. Sons and daughters still love and respect their parents to the full, but as dear friends and equals—not the source of authority and security. Nor does the untying of apron strings mean that adolescents should be indifferent to the advice of their home folks. Instead they value it highly, and listen to it. But as they move down through the teens, they should be increasingly able to stand off and weigh all such counsel impartially and form their own judgments in the light of everything that seems true and good.

At the end, we see a group of mature individuals meeting on a plane of equality. Each loves the other, not because he needs to but because he has found something in the other worth loving. Each respects the other, not because he has to but because the other deserves his respect. Each is free to live his own life and to be himself, and yet remains attached to every other in the family circle in a grown-up and wholesome manner.

The most important achievement of the adolescent years, in which both generations must join, is the proper untying of the apron strings.

We are members one of another.

—EPHESIANS 4: 25

6

GETTING ALONG WITH OTHERS

I would be true, for there are those who trust me;
I would be pure, for there are those who care;
I would be strong, for there is much to suffer;
I would be brave, for there is much to dare.

I would be friend of all—the foe, the friendless;
I would be giving, and forget the gift;
I would be humble, for I know my weakness;
I would look up, and laugh, and love, and lift.

—HOWARD ARNOLD WALTER

IT MAY be that on our first reading of *Robinson Crusoe* we envied him his peaceful life on his private island inhabited only by parrots, goats, and himself. Nobody to bother him! Nobody to claim a part of the food he painstakingly raised, or of the supplies he salvaged from the wrecked ship offshore! But it must have become very tiresome, for he was overjoyed when he saw the footprints of his man Friday on the beach. After all, parrots and goats leave something to be desired as companions. And we were not meant to live alone. Instead, "we are members one of another." We belong to each other.

As we have already seen, nothing gives us greater satisfaction than to be in with the gang, and to be sure of our place in it. And nothing cuts us more deeply than unpopularity. On every count, it is important to be able to get along with others. Our present happiness depends upon it. Our future usefulness depends upon it. In many vocations the ability to meet people easily and work with them well is essential to success. And even our Christian discipleship depends upon it. For we are reminded again and again that the whole duty of a Christian consists of finding a right relation with God, and with his fellowmen; and that we can't do the first unless we also do the second.

Almost nothing gives young people more concern than getting along well with others. They think about it, worry over it, and work hard at it. "How to Make Friends" is a topic of major interest in youth groups. Are there any rules to guide us in this matter? If so, what are they?

What Do We Like in Others?

Perhaps this is as good a way to begin as any. Call to mind three or four persons whom you like very much. Or else select a few young people who are highly popular in school, summer camp, church school, or youth fellowship. What are they like? How would you describe them? Do most of them have something in common, which might be the secret of their popularity? How close is the following to a thumbnail sketch of the kind of persons we and others like?

1. *We like people who are interesting.* Who doesn't? Such people are fun. We enjoy being with them. Our spirits lift a notch when we see them coming. As for their opposite—well, the names change from one period to another. A generation ago it was "poor fish." Today it is "drip" or "droop." What it will be a generation from now, no one knows, but the types remain the same. And interesting people are always welcome in any company. Let us try, therefore, to break this notion down a little, and see what it is made of.

Interesting people have a sense of humor. They can see the funny side of things. They don't take either themselves or life with such deadly seriousness that they can't laugh a little as they go along. They can tell a joke, play a joke, and take a joke. Abraham Lincoln with all his greatness—perhaps as a part of his greatness—possessed a saving sense of humor. When he

73

was asked to give an inventory of the assets of a young lawyer, he replied in this vein: "He has a wife and baby who ought to be worth a million dollars to any man; a slightly dilapidated desk and chair adorn his law office; and over in the corner is a rat-hole which would bear looking into." No wonder that people not only revered him, but also liked him!

Interesting people enjoy life. They get a kick out of it as they go along. They find it good, no matter how many sorrows and disappointments it contains. When the sun is shining, they act as though there never had been such brilliant sunshine since the world began; and when it is raining, they look forward to the time when the sun will come out again. To them, the world is chock-full of interest. They are like Robert Louis Stevenson, who despite ill health and much suffering could say:

> The world is so full of a number of things,
> I'm sure we should all be as happy as kings.

A run-down house along the road sets them wondering how old it is, and why the roof was pitched so high. An automobile must be examined to see what can be said for or against that new type of radiator grill. A coffee cup is just like one that Aunt Sarah had; or is it a little bit different? A bird singing in a tree outside the window calls for a thorough investigation. And so on with everything and everyone they meet! Life is one continuous adventure.

Interesting people can do interesting things. They swim, sing, skate, dance, sew, read, collect stamps, draw, hike, act, and so on and on. No one of them can do all these things, but each one of them can do some. A certain young minister was quite popular as a camp leader. In addition to being a good teacher, he liked to hike. He played a fair game of baseball. He was quite at home in craft work. He was an excellent naturalist, being well acquainted with many species of birds, plants, and trees. And the things he couldn't do—why, he simply enjoyed his blundering efforts there as much as everyone else did. He couldn't swim worth a cent, and his spread-eagle dives were something to behold, but he merely laughed at himself as heartily as the spectators laughed at him. As a result, people young and old liked to be with him.

These are some of the marks of an interesting person, the kind we like.

2. *We like people who are interested in us.* We care little for those who insist on talking about themselves all the time. In fact, a bore has been defined as a person who talks about himself when you want to talk about yourself. But let a new acquaintance begin to inquire about our home or car or school or hobbies, and we suddenly conclude that this is one of the most remarkably discerning and interesting people we have ever met.

A college freshman at the tender age of seventeen once went on a double date with a fraternity brother. In the course of the evening he treated the party to a long discourse on some of the highlights of his own previous career. He told in detail about some trips he and his family had taken, the remarkable performance of the family car on some formidable hills, the clever remarks tossed off by his father and his brother at one point or another along the road, and even the unusual lunches which they had enjoyed under that big tree just south of the bridge over the south fork of the river. The whole account was extremely fascinating—to him. He had the time of his life, and was quite well satisfied with himself by the time the evening was over. The rude awakening came a few days later, when he overheard his fraternity brother regaling some of the other brethren with the whole story, complete with the exact gestures and voice inflections he had used. Instead of creating quite an impression, he had merely succeeded in making himself ridiculous.

No, the people we like best are those who take an interest in us. They are not so taken up with themselves as to leave no room for us. On the contrary, they take us into their attention, their conversation, and their plans. They make us feel that we count. They heighten our sense of our own worth. They bring us out. As a consequence, we enjoy being with them, and regard them as most likable people.

How well does all this fit your own best friends? Are these the reasons why you like them, and are happy to count them as your friends? How well does the foregoing description fit the most popular people you know? Does this explain their popularity? You will notice that we have said nothing about good character—honesty, decency, and the like. Qualities such as these are of the utmost importance in ourselves and in our friends. But we are not asking now what sort of person we admire. We are putting one simple question: Whom do we like?

What Do Others Like in Us?

It takes only a little thought to realize that the answers here are exactly the same as they were before. Indeed it would be very strange if this were not the case, since all of us are alike and have very much the same likes and dislikes.

1. *Others like us when we are interesting.*

They take to people with a sense of humor. (How do we measure up?)

They seek out people who enjoy life. (Do we leave the impression that life is to us a rich and enjoyable affair?)

They gravitate toward people who can do interesting things. (How many can we do?)

2. *Others like us when we are interested in them.*

They prefer to be with people who do not think about themselves all the time. (How much of our conversation is about ourselves? How much about the other fellow? How much about something outside us all which is equally appealing to all of us?)

These are rather pointed questions. We might wish that we could avoid them. But they are merely our own likes and dis-

likes, turned around and headed in our direction. Do you think
they give a true picture of what others like in us? If so, note
what they leave out.

We do not have to own a convertible in order to be popular.

We do not have to spend money like water.

We do not have to look like Clark Gable, or Rita Hayworth.

We do not have to wear expensive clothes.

We do not have to be brilliant, a "brain."

We do not have to look with scorn upon good, honest study.

We do not have to dance like an Arthur Murray instructor.

We do not have to break any athletic records.

We do not have to swear, cheat, or drink.

We do not have to poke fun at home, school, church, God,
or duty.

We do not have to spend seven nights a week downtown with
the gang.

To be perfectly honest, certain items in this list may carry some
weight in groups that you know. But can you not think of boys
and girls who are quite popular without them?

How to Become Likable

Here is one of those goals in life that can't be achieved by
going at it directly. We can't simply say: "Now I am going to
be likable. I am going to make myself popular." The most probable result of tackling the matter in this way is just the opposite,
namely, to become a laughing-stock. It is worth while, of course,
to give some careful thought to popularity and how it comes,
as we are doing in this chapter. But all this can accomplish is
to clear away any misconceptions, and locate the crucial points
that need attention. Beyond this, the less we think about the
matter, the better. For the more we aim at popularity directly,
the more we miss it. The harder we try, the farther short we
fall of what we hope to accomplish. What is needed is a flank
attack, not a frontal attack.

The first step in this indirect approach is to develop an out-going interest in life. This should not be too hard, for there are so many fascinating things to do, see, learn, and enjoy. They are all ready and waiting for you. So, if you would like to be likable, forget about it, and turn your attention away from yourself to things outside you. It can be anything from algebra to be-bop; from religious art to roller skating. Of course, it goes without saying that the higher the interest, the better it will be for you. Shakespeare, for example, is scarcely to be mentioned in the same breath with the comics. Also, an interest that can be shared with others is generally to be preferred to one of the "lone eagle" type. Bridge is better in this respect than solitaire, and basketball than weight lifting. But the important thing is to get outside yourself, and get yourself off your hands. And interests will do the trick!

As you follow them, and lose yourself in them, a number of things will begin to happen. You will find that you are less self-conscious. You think less about yourself. You talk less about yourself. Furthermore, you are happier. You have more to live for. Some of these activities are of interest also to others. You can talk about them with your friends, and do them jointly with a companion or a group. And, the first thing you know, you are an interesting person. Others like you. While you were concentrating on these outgoing interests, the capacity for friendship came sneaking in the back door. That is the way it always happens.

The second step in this indirect approach is to develop an out-going interest in other people. Of course this must be genuine, for a sham feeling for others which is turned on for the occasion is worse than nothing. But the real thing should not prove at all difficult. For other persons are interesting. As someone has said, "People are more fun than anybody." They do such strange things, and make such funny remarks. What are they like—these people who are all around you? What are they hoping, fearing, and secretly worrying about? Here is a little

78

child next door, who is something of a nuisance. How does life look to him? Have you ever given the matter much thought? Or your teacher, who stands before you every day. What would it be like to be in her shoes? Or a classmate, with whom you have grown up. How much do you really know about him (or her)?

As you concentrate in this way upon other people, something will happen to you. If by any chance you have been spoiled a trifle, and somewhat wrapped up in yourself, you will find your selfishness and self-concern slipping off you like an overcoat from your shoulders. You will be happier, and easier to live with. As you concern yourself naturally and sympathetically with others, they will respond. They will like to be with you. If you happen to notice it, you will realize that you have become likable. While you were thinking about someone else, the capacity for friendship tiptoed quietly in through the back door. It always happens that way.

Two Main Obstacles

This is the main outline of the recipe for becoming likable. But it may be in order to give a little thought to two main obstacles which often stand in the way, namely, being spoiled, and being self-conscious. Both have been mentioned, but only briefly.

The spoiled person is often none too likable—and that is putting it mildly! He may have grown up as the only child in the family. Only children are not invariably spoiled by any means, but with two parents, four grandparents, and assorted aunts and uncles all revolving around one baby the chances of being spoiled are fairly good. Or he may have been sickly, and thus received a little more attention than was best for him. Or perhaps he is good, and knows it. The willing and capable youth, who is chairman of everything at school and president of everything at church, is under strong temptation to think of himself as the center of the universe. At all events, the spoiled person may not be a well liked or completely likable companion.

What is to be done in such a case? Unfortunately, it is not quite enough for him to tighten up his will power, and say, "I am not going to be spoiled." Rather let him think back over what has made him as he is, realize that anyone else going through the same experiences would have come out the same way, smile a little at himself—and then turn his attention outward. If a play is being given, for example, he might get so lost in the play itself that he would volunteer for the humble task of assembling stage properties, which would never bring him before the footlights or even get his name on the program. If an election of officers is being held, he might treat himself to the fun of nominating someone else for the presidency, and enjoy the look of satisfaction on the other's face. Strange how "spiledness" evaporates under such treatment!

The self-conscious person, too, is often none too likable (although he is frequently much more popular than he thinks). Certainly he is none too happy in a crowd. He is painfully aware of every move he makes, and every word he says. Everybody seems to be staring at him, and he can't get himself out of mind. This sort of thing generally has a long history of inferiority-feeling, beginning away back in childhood. Perhaps he had a brother or sister who was bigger, brighter, more attractive, or better loved by his parents than he was. Later at school and in play he took many a beating, both figuratively and literally. Now he can't think of anything but himself, and is quite ill at ease with others of his own age.

What is a self-conscious person to do? Obviously there is nothing to be gained by repeating ten times daily, "I am not going to be self-conscious." That merely makes matters worse. Instead, let him try to understand how he got to be as he is, comfort himself with the thought that anyone else following the same path would have come out at the same point, laugh a little at the whole silly business—and then turn his attention outward. If he is out for basketball, the team as a whole and the game itself are the things to think about. If he thinks about them hard enough, he will forget that he is there. At a party, the kindest thing he can do for himself is to single out some wallflower and see to it that he (or she) has a good time that evening. When he stands before a group to speak and his hands and feet seem at least three feet long, the way out is to concentrate hard on what he wants to say and the reactions of the people before him. Lo! the self-consciousness disappears somewhere, and he becomes happier, more useful, and more likable.

There used to be quack doctors who went around selling medicines guaranteed to cure almost anything—backache, tuberculosis, spots before the eyes, heartburn, indigestion, fallen arches, and general weakness. We now know that there is no such medicine. But in the realm of personality there is one prescription which has marvelous properties. It will give eventual if not instant relief in cases of being spoiled, or being self-conscious; and it is also guaranteed to make a person happier, more popular, and even more Christian. It consists simply of thinking of something and someone outside oneself. Jesus gave this same prescription most clearly a long time ago: "For whoever would save his life will lose it; and whoever loses his life for my sake and the gospel's will save it" (Mark 9: 35).

When the Gang Is Wrong

In our great eagerness for popularity, there is a strong tendency to go along with the crowd in whatever it does. But sometimes the gang is wrong; we are sure it is. What then?

The first question to be asked is whether or not it is really wrong. Dancing and card playing, for instance, may be all right, provided they are done rightly. We are not called upon to stand out against others on issues that are trivial or even false. But reckless drinking, dangerous driving, heavy and promiscuous petting, and wasting countless precious hours on the drugstore corner are clearly wrong. And there are some prices too heavy to pay for popularity.

We may derive some comfort from the fact—and it is a fact!
—that the person who is thoroughly likable in some of the
basic respects we have mentioned can get away with a good
deal of independence on moral standards, and still be popular.
The happy-go-lucky girl who can sing a little, dance a little,
skate a little, and generally prove to be an enjoyable companion, can be altogether decent and not forfeit her popularity.
The boy who says "Hello" to everybody and at the same time
holds the school record in the hundred-yard dash can refrain
from smoking, drinking, and anything else he feels he should
refrain from, and still carry the school around with him in his
vest pocket.

Beyond this, there are only two things to do.

The one is to find another gang. There is almost always one
available. It may be, and often is, at church. Fortunate is the
young person who finds in his church school class or youth
fellowship a group which is congenial, enjoyable, and possessed
of high standards of attitude or conduct. If he anchors himself
in that, he is all right.

The other is to start one's own. If we quietly stand our
ground "without looking too good or talking too wise," we
may find others rallying around our standard. It requires some
strength and courage, but youth has both. Twenty-five years
hence we may find ourselves much happier than those we now
envy for their cheap popularity.

Happy is the man that findeth wisdom.

—PROVERBS 3:13

7

SCHOOL IS WHAT YOU MAKE IT

Take us on the Quest of Knowledge
Clearest Thinker man has known;
Make our minds sincere and patient,
Satisfied by Truth alone.

Take us on the Quest of Service,
Kingly Servant of man's need,
Let us work with Thee for others,
Anywhere Thy purpose leads.

All along our Quest's far pathways,
Christ our Leader and our guide,
Make us conscious of Thy presence,
Walking always at our side.

—ELEANOR B. STOCK
Used by permission of the author.

A THOUSAND YEARS ago in Europe it would have been of little consequence whether you made much of school or not. Only the privileged few went to school at all, while for most people life proceeded on its way without benefit of formal education. Consequently, you might have attended a little while and dropped out, or never gone at all, without any marked effect on your present or your future.

But here and now the situation is altogether different. Everybody is in school through the years required by law, and an increasing number beyond the end of this period. During the formative period of your life you spend six hours a day, five days a week, nine to ten months a year in school. This is your first real contact with the world of success or failure. There-

83

fore, both your present and your future happiness depend in large measure on how well you make out at school.

Why Some Pupils Fail

Let us consider six imaginary individuals, all of whom are on the borderline of flunking. Each one represents a real cause of failure which is often found in actual life.

Student A tries his level best, but can't make decent grades. In class he pays strict attention, hanging pathetically on every word spoken by the teacher or his fellow pupils. Each evening he settles down to two or three hours of painstaking study. His reports are always turned in on time, and they are generally lengthy and detailed. But despite all his efforts, he comes out consistently with a row of C's and D's. If the truth were known, as it probably is to his teachers, his mental abilities do not equip him well for academic work. In many other respects he may be admirably fitted for a rich and useful life. Conceivably he is honest, likable, and dependable. If an automobile is needed to take a swimming team to a meet in a distant city, you can be sure that he will turn up at the appointed place on time with everything ready, and will provide safe and efficient transportation. In fact, he may be very much at home with machinery, and highly skilled in its use. But in general intelligence, the kind of ability that most courses require, he is below average. He is competing in a realm for which he is not well suited, like a two hundred and fifty pound man trying to run the hundred-yard dash. In all probability he should not plan to go on to college. And even now he might be more successful in a different sort of curriculum.

Student B's report card also breaks out in a rash of C's and D's, but for just the opposite reason. He is too bright to fit well into the ordinary classroom. For, unless he is attending a large school where the pupils can be grouped according to ability, the work of his class is pitched at the level of the average student. And that is too low for Student B. He finds little to challenge him. The problems are too easy. The questions are too simple. Without really exerting himself, he finishes everything before the majority of the class is through. Then he has time to burn—and burn it he does. He may feel called upon to talk with a pretty girl sitting near him, or raise his hand for a question that strikes the teacher as being impertinent, or set his active mind to work on some novel kind of mischief. By and by both the teacher and the class get down on him, and school becomes unappealing. His work moves from bad to worse, until he may actually tremble on the verge of failure because he is too bright. The remedy lies in finding harder individual tasks for him, which will stretch the muscles of his mind.

Student C is a puzzle both to himself and to his teachers. He appears bright enough, but for some reason or other he frequently fails to hear what is going on in class. The pages to be read for the next day are clearly specified, but when he gets home he finds that he doesn't know what the assignment is. Or the teacher spends fifteen minutes elaborating a certain point, but the next day the whole matter is blank to him. Naturally the teacher is impatient with him, and he is somewhat put out with himself. Everything sounds like a low, indistinct rumble, but for all he knows it sounds the same way to everyone else. Finally he goes to a doctor, and discovers to his amazement that he is partially deaf. Now it is all clear. The vague rumble to which he has been listening for many years is to others a set of perfectly distinct sounds. If his defective hearing can be cured, or improved with a hearing aid, he suddenly enters a new world—and begins to do far better work. The same thing can happen, of course, in the realm of vision. Quite a few children and young people are thus handicapped without knowing it. Even if they suspect that something is wrong, they may hesitate to speak about it for fear of appearing foolish.

Student D doesn't see much sense in the usual school subjects. Why, for example, should he bother to learn French? If the people of France insist on talking through their noses, let them go to it; but that is no reason why he should bother with their strange language. History is just a rehashing of the dead past. What difference does it make who licked whom a hundred and fifty years ago? It's all settled now, and there's nothing we can do about it. And as for mathematics, who cares what the value of x is in the equation, $4x + 3y = 12$? Or how many rolls of wall-paper it takes to cover a room 12 by 15 by 10 with two windows on the one side and a single window on the other? It all leaves him cold. But music—now that is a different matter! He listens to every concert he can hear, and plays records incessantly. Furthermore, his violin is his pride and joy, and he spends many happy hours with it. But in school they don't pay off on music; it is French, history, algebra, and the like that count. And so, try as hard as he may, he can't work up any great enthusiasm for school. As a result, his standing is poor. He belongs to the minority of talented youth whose abilities and interests lie along specialized lines, and who consequently do not find the standardized school curriculum to their liking.

Student E comes to school each morning from a tense and quarrelsome home. He can't help it that his mother and father don't get along well, but he can't avoid being affected by it. All day long the memory of those bitter words at the breakfast table hangs over him. If he does succeed in shaking it off for a little while, sooner or later it returns. As the day wears on, the hour draws closer when he must go home again. More fights! More scoldings! More unhappiness! But this is the only home he has, and there is no escape. It is little wonder, then, that his mind is only half on books and recitations. The other half is busy worrying. Maybe the teacher addresses a question to him just when he is trying to figure the whole business out, and he doesn't have any idea what she is talking about. Naturally that doesn't endear him to the teacher, or give him any reason to be proud of himself. And so his unhappiness increases, and his grades go down. He is caught in a vicious circle. The music goes round and round, and comes out nowhere. Quite a few boys and girls are handicapped at school simply by emotional tension. It may come from conditions at home, some disappointment at school, or a secret worry which they wouldn't tell a soul. Whatever it is, it uses up part of their time and energy, and shaves many points off their school standing.

Student F suffers from poor work habits. Call him lazy, or careless, or fun-crazy, or happy-go-lucky, or harum scarum, or anything you like; the simple truth is that he has never learned to work consistently, and isn't too anxious to learn now. The chances are he has no particular goal ahead for which to prepare. The present is all he bothers about. He isn't much good at organizing his time, or himself. In fact, he is a stranger to self-discipline. This thing of setting aside a certain period for regular study doesn't appeal to him in the least. Why bother about books when there's something going on? And there's always something going on! And why do something on Monday? Aren't Thursday and Friday coming along soon? That will be plenty of time. Thus the days and the weeks pass by quite pleasantly, but nothing much gets done. Finally the day of reckoning arrives, generally in the form of a final examination. One such boy simply wandered off one evening before high school examination and didn't show up again for three years. He had joined the Navy. In most cases the ending is not quite so dramatic, but it is just as certain. Whatever a person sows, he reaps in due time.

Learning How to Study

No one is born with the ability to study well. Rather it is an art which has to be learned precisely like any other highly developed skill—playing the pipe organ, driving an automobile, or swimming the back stroke. It is a hard thing to pin down in phrases and sentences. If you really want to do effective study, how are you to go at it? Do the following rules or suggestions offer any practical help?

Try to find something interesting and important in every-thing you study. This is the first and great commandment. For no one is going to study well and long unless he finds some fascination in it and sees some point to it. Suppose, for example, you are studying the Revolutionary War in history class; you can begin asking yourself all sorts of questions about it. Why was it fought? Why did it come just when it did, and not in 1750 or 1825? Why did Canada not go through a like struggle for independence at the same time? Why did we win? What would have happened if we had lost? Who were the chief leaders on both sides, and what sort of people were they? How much trouble did the thirteen Colonies have in becoming the United States? Does this throw any light on the struggle in the twentieth century to organize effectively the United Nations? And so on through a host of queries, which will make this period come alive to you and fill it with interest and significance.

Or take the study of plane geometry. How many theorems can you find that have the number three in them? Why are there so many more with the number two? Why is it so easy to bisect an angle, and so hard to trisect one? The same thing can be done with language. Why, for example, did Latin come out with seven different cases, while English gets along with only three? And what do we do when we want to express some-thing for which Latin uses a dative or an ablative? And wasn't it a strange oversight on the part of the ancient Romans that they never developed any definite articles? What substitutes did they use? And why is it that in the Romance languages there is a "gu" in words such as "guerre" and "Guillaume," while in the Germanic tongues a "w" shows up in the same spot ("war" and "William")? How did the one get changed into the other? Do both go back to a common root, and, if so, what is it? In chemistry too there is endless room for questions. In common table salt (NaCl) one atom of sodium combines with one atom of chlorine to form a molecule of salt. Why is it one of each? Baking soda also contains sodium, but it is quite different from salt. In what ways is it different? And what makes the difference? Why does sulphur form one type of crystals if it cools at a certain temperature, and another type if it cools at a different temperature? Why are some compounds stable, while others fall apart if you say "Boo" at them?

The idea, then, is to let your mind play actively over all the material you study, like flashes of lightning darting back and forth across the landscape. If to this you can add some insight into how these studies link up with the profession you expect to follow or the life you plan to live, you will have taken the first long step toward effective study.

Learn to read rapidly and well. A great many people read slowly and inefficiently, and get no more out of their effort than if they moved considerably faster—perhaps not so much! There is such a thing as paying so much attention to each separate tree as to miss the forest; so much attention to each word as to miss the sentence; so much attention to each sentence as to miss the paragraph. At the end there is a confused jumble of impressions from many parts, but no clear impression of the whole passage. What is needed is a faster movement and a wider sweep in our reading.

There are, of course, some outstanding exceptions to this rule. If you are reading masterful poetry or prose, whose worth lies chiefly in the way the words are put together, you may well take your time and "taste" every line to the full. No one, for example, would think of tearing through Lincoln's Gettysburg Address with a view only to the main point it makes. There is much more to it than its main point. Likewise, when you come to a section heading, or a rule written in italics, or a compact summary at the end of a chapter, such reading is to be done slowly, thoughtfully, minutely, carefully. You will gain in the end if you take plenty of time at such points; for they either signal what is coming, or sum up what has already been set forth. Also, when you stumble upon a word whose meaning you do not know, it is well to take time out and look it up.

It will pay you in the long run to do so; for you will both make sure of understanding what you are now reading and enlarge your vocabulary for future reading. Many students keep a good, not too large dictionary right at their elbows all the time, and use it constantly.

But these are exceptions, and the rule itself still stands. For all ordinary reading, look for the main idea in a whole sentence, and the central point in a whole paragraph. Accelerate your pace. Press a little. Even skim a little, after you have had some practice. You may find that you will be able to cut your reading time for a history assignment one-fourth or one-third, and actually know more about the chapter when you have finished than you would have known if you had labored over it too much bit by bit. In the time thus saved, you can go back over it again, noting the highlights, reviewing in your own words the major points, nailing down significant dates and personages, and making it your own.

Organize what you read and hear. Nobody can easily remember 1, 6, 7, 2, 4. But anyone can instantly memorize 1, 3, 5, 7, 9. What is the difference? There is no rhyme or reason to the first series. No inner connection holds the several numbers together. They don't fit into any framework. But the second series is a different matter. The items are the first five odd numbers. An interval of two separates them in each case. They hang together. They are interrelated. Hence they can be readily learned, and long remembered. Without any further study, you could repeat them next week if you wanted to. But not the first series!

Therefore, a major essential of good study is the knack of organizing. All sorts of ways exist for doing this in your head or on paper. One is the familiar outline-form. If you are studying the causes of America's break with England in the eighteenth century, arrange the different items in an outline. Point 1 might be the political causes, with (a), (b), and (c) under that. Point 2 would then be the economic causes, with its own (a), (b), and (c). And so on until you have everything important packed into a succinct outline. Or, for some purposes, you may prefer a series of parallel columns. For example, if you are trying to comprehend the workings of our federal government, you can put the executive functions into one column, the legislative into a second, and the judicial into a third. What might otherwise be a mass of unrelated, meaningless items will now be clear, meaningful, and far easier to remember.

Yet another useful way of organizing a subject is to keep a file of 3 x 5 cards, on which you have entered whatever seems to you most important. If you are building up your vocabulary in a foreign language such as German, you can make out a card for each new word, listing the principal parts if it is a verb, or the gender if it is a noun, plus any similar English words, or anything else worth noting. When these are arranged alphabetically, you have a useful tool for your purpose. In the same way, the main laws of physics, the major rules of grammar, or the chief events in a certain period of history can be made into card files. A half dozen that belong together naturally can be fastened together with a paper clip, or marked with the same distinctive color in the upper right-hand corner. You can shuffle through them for review purposes, and at all times you have the main essentials at your finger tips. There is a good deal of fun in making such a device, and a most comfortable feeling when it is done.

Relate everything to something else. Nobody can get very far in mastering and remembering a great number of unrelated facts. But associate them one with another, and the task becomes not only possible but even enjoyable.

For example, imagine that you are studying Latin, and come for the first time in your life upon the word "miles" (soldier). At first it is merely a strange combination of five letters. It doesn't mean a thing. It may even look like the plural of the English word "mile." Before it can be understood, remembered, and used, it must be linked with something. And so you begin.

Here is the familiar word "military"; also "militant"; also "militate"; not to mention "militia." All of them look very much like "miles." As a matter of fact, they are all derived from this Latin root. Now the new word is no longer strange. It has meaning. You can remember it. You have associated it with something else.

Or you are studying Shakespeare, and want to get him straightened out in time and space. Where did he live? At Stratford, a little country town on the Avon river not too far north of Oxford. When did he live? 1564-1616. What was going on in England at the time? For one thing, the Stuarts came into power during the latter part of his life. For another, the King James translation of the Bible was made during his lifetime. What was going on in America? The Indians had it all to themselves during most of his life. Christopher Columbus had died not many years before he was born. Did Shakespeare have any knowledge of the New World? And so you put this over against that, until not only Shakespeare but a number of other matters fill up with new meaning. And, when it is finished, you won't soon forget when and where Shakespeare lived.

Discipline yourself to good study habits. The first step here is to secure as good a place as possible. A radio doesn't help greatly, and a television set even less. And a constant flow of family conversation doesn't mix well with the binomial theorem. Next in order are the tools of your trade—a desk or table (if it is only a card table) on which you can lay out your books and papers; a comfortable chair, but not too comfortable; a good light; a dictionary, map, or whatever else you need. These are the working equipment. They are as essential to the student as a work bench is to the mechanic. Then set a schedule for yourself, one that is airtight save for exceptional circumstances. If study is important, certain hours must be kept for it—just as for basketball practice—and kept regularly without fail. Then pitch in! If it isn't easy the first time, it will be easier the twenty-first time. Above all, form the habit of keeping up to

92

date with your work. If you fall behind, you lose the foundation on which succeeding days build. When a person has once got the hang of consistent, effective study, there is real joy in it. And twenty-five years later the rewards are even greater.

Things Not Found in Books

Jane and Joan are sisters, but there the resemblance stops. Jane is a student. You might even call her a bookworm. She lives for study, and little else. Each night she carries home a back-breaking load of books, and each new day she dazzles everyone with the brilliance of her knowledge. For Joan, on the other hand, the curriculum is strictly secondary. It is the extra-curricular activities which are her chief interest. She seems to be in everything. She is a cheer leader, a member of the school chorus, the chairman of half the dance committees at the school, vice-president of the photography club, and secretary of the student council. If and when she has nothing else to do, she studies.

Which is better off, Jane or Joan? Neither! Both are one-sided.

There is much to be gained from school outside the covers of books. Indeed many persons feel that "extracurricular" is a poor term for the clubs and activities which play so large a part in modern education. They are not "outside the curriculum," but a true part of it. A student may learn more music in the school orchestra than from a course in music appreciation, and more English as a reporter on the school paper than from a class in composition. But he learns other things also which are of the utmost importance in later life, such as the ability to get along well with others, and a wholesome measure of self-confidence. Without these, mere book-learning can be largely empty and useless.

But it still remains true that much can be said for good, honest study. A faithful student not merely lays a sound foundation of knowledge for whatever study or vocation he wishes to

93

pursue later, but—perhaps more important!—he establishes the habit of conscientious work. The facts he learns at seventeen may be largely forgotten by the time he is fifty, but the habit of doing the best work of which he is capable will probably still be with him. One college studied the later careers of its alumni to see whether there was any connection between their standing in college and their subsequent success in life. There was! Old-fashioned or not, to be a good student is still worth while.

How Long Shall I Stay in School?

It goes without saying that, barring very unusual circumstances, every young person nowadays ought to continue his education up to the point of graduation from high school. Beyond that lie nursing school, technical training, college, and professional or graduate school. Many a boy or girl asks sooner or later, "Are these for me?" As in so many cases, the answer is, "It depends."

First of all, what do you want to be in life? Most of the professions and many of the better opportunities in business require at least a college education. Some other honorable ways of making a living do not.

Secondly, what are the financial resources of yourself and your family? In a period of rising prices, higher education like everything else is increasingly expensive. However, many scholarships are available for capable students. And there are numerous opportunities for work, not only in the summer but also during the academic year. A reasonable amount of such work does the student no harm, either in his health or in his scholarship. And in most colleges self-help is a badge of honor.

In the third place, how well have you got along in school thus far? If your grades are low, you probably should consider something other than college, unless you have real ability which you have not been using to the full thus far and are sure you can give a better account of it in the future.

94

Notice that nothing has been said to the effect that a young person ought to plan to go to college in order to make more money in life. A college graduate may or may not be better off financially than the industrial worker who has not had a higher education. The advantages of college lie rather in other fields. They are to be found not primarily in higher salary, but in necessary preparation for some vocation which the person greatly desires, and in the greater richness of life which is open to those with more years of formal education. A wife and mother who has never earned one cent as a result of going to college may still judge it worth her time and effort. She is a better wife and mother; she appreciates life more; she puts more into it and gets more out of it because of her four years at college.

Finally, whether you go on to school or not after high school commencement, you can continue to learn and grow as long as you live. There are books, lectures, concerts, plays, church classes, community forums which provide ceaseless opportunities for developing mind, heart, and spirit. To live is to learn; and to learn is to live fully.

Therefore shall a man leave his father and his mother, and shall cleave unto his wife: and they shall be one flesh.

—GENESIS 2: 24

8

BOY MEETS GIRL

The wild hawk to the wind-swept sky,
The deer to the wholesome wold
And the heart of a man to the heart of a maid,
As it was in the days of old.

The heart of a man to the heart of a maid—
Light of my tents, be fleet.
Morning waits at the end of the world,
And the world is all at our feet!

—From "The Gipsy Trail" from *Rudyard Kipling's Verse,* Inclusive Edition. Reprinted by permission of Mrs. George Bambridge and Doubleday & Company, Inc.

LITTLE BOYS and girls play together in kindergarten at the same games with the same toys, and show little awareness of sex differences. In later childhood they pass through a period when boys group together, and girls do the same, and each is rather scornful of the other—or pretends to be. Then around the age of thirteen or fourteen a new stage begins. The sexes become attractive to each other. Significant bodily changes take place. The reproductive organs develop, and start to function. The girl rounds out into a woman. The boy's voice turns husky, a fuzz appears on his face, and he becomes a man. The truth of the matter is that their bodies are getting ready for marriage and parenthood later on. And, along with these physical developments, come certain emotional changes also. In general, adolescents can feel more deeply about a number of things than they could before. In particular, they are sharply drawn toward members of the opposite sex. A whole new set of emotional interests comes into play.

The way is now open for some of the richest joys or deepest sorrows, depending upon how these new urges and relationships are handled.

Puppy Love

Some wag has said that puppy love is the beginning of a dog's life. One implication is that these initial love affairs commonly ripen into engagement and marriage. But this is not a true picture of the situation at all. Most of the romances which begin in the early or middle teens do not end before an altar. The chances are that your parents or any other married couple you know did not start going together when they were fifteen. Possibly they did, but probably they didn't. At fifteen in all likelihood it was someone else, whom they may not have seen during the past twenty-five years, and who would not start any heart throbs now but merely a puzzled recollection. No, puppy love is not as a rule the first direct step toward marriage and a home. Nevertheless, it means a great deal to those who are going through it. In order to understand it, we must trace what happens to individuals as they cross over the threshold from childhood to youth.

Some few go down through the teens almost as though the opposite sex weren't around. They don't date. They don't show up in mixed groups any more than they have to. They merely stick to themselves, or else to their own sex. Here is a boy, for example, who carries a prominent birthmark on his face, and hesitates to approach the girls on that account. Or a girl who is so painfully self-conscious in all her social contacts that she gets flustered whenever a boy comes near her. Or an adolescent so closely tied to mother's or father's apron strings that he or she is not emotionally free to seek out other persons of the

97

opposite sex. Young people in situations such as these do not have an easy row to hoe. They are often genuinely unhappy, although they may try to hide this fact both from themselves and from others. In later years they may succeed in making a better adjustment with the other half of the human family, or they may not. Perhaps if they tried now they would find it easier than they think.

A good many go on month after month without striking up any attachment with any particular boy or girl. They like them all. They enjoy going to the movies in a mixed crowd, or laughing and talking with boys and girls together, and feel very much at home. They have dates every now and then, but it is one person this week and another person next week, and it doesn't make too much difference who it is—as long as it is someone of the opposite sex. This is a pretty good arrangement. Of course, it has to change sooner or later, but there is no need to rush the matter.

Still others pair off more definitely at an earlier stage in the game. There is some indication that boys gravitate first of all toward tomboyish girls, and then turn toward those who are more frilly and feminine. Girls on the other hand soon begin to prefer boys a little older than themselves, which is as it should be, because they mature earlier and are really as old at fourteen as their supposed lords and masters are at sixteen. At any rate, the teen-agers of whom we are now thinking find themselves going around two by two. This first romance is likely to be highly romantic, just because it is the first. It is the initial taste of a brand new experience, which may be repeated several times over during the coming years. But, as far as they now know, it is the only love affair that ever was or ever will be. It is definitely out of this world. They walk around halfway between heaven and earth. The other person is the most wonderful, talented, and attractive creature ever to grace this planet. And the mysterious bond which links them together is unspeakably strong and beautiful. What has actually happened is that each has fallen in love partly with the other, and partly with the idea of falling in love.

This sort of early romantic experience, which comes to some adolescents but not to all, is not to be ridiculed in any sense. It means too much to the boy and girl for that. And, if kept within proper bounds, it can serve a good purpose. It is a foretaste of the love which binds a man and woman together inseparably. For the present it lifts the passing hours to new heights of emotional richness (although it does get in the way sometimes of basketball and algebra). And it provides each one with practical, first-hand knowledge of the opposite sex. As Kipling makes his roving lover say, "I learned about women from 'er!" Thirty years later the boy may not even remember the name of the girl who was the embodiment of everything lovely. And the girl, upon meeting a bald-headed man with a bulge at his waistline, may wonder if this can be the boy for whom she waited after school with such impatient delight.

The Problem of Petting

The starting point for Christians in approaching this problem which torments young people a good deal is the principle that we are more than bodies. Each of us is a body-soul complex, which is a strange name to give a pretty girl or a handsome boy, but it happens to be the truth. Our bodies are a legitimate part of us. They come from the hand of God. They deserve proper care and attention. And they are not sinful, neither they nor the strange urges and desires which arise within them. But they are not all of us. They are not the most important part of us. We are also personalities, spirits, souls, or whatever name you wish to use, which can think, and dream, and aspire, and sacrifice, and fellowship with God and man, and live forever.

Any way of acting, therefore, which treats persons as though they were merely bodies and nothing more, is wrong. Slavery was wrong for this very reason. It put a human being on the auction block, pinched his muscles and examined his teeth, and largely forgot the rest of him. Industry is wrong whenever it sees persons as bodies and nothing more. One of the reasons why war seems wrong to many people is that the battlefield tends to reduce human beings to bodies and to forget their spirits. Even a handshake is wrong, if it doesn't mean what it "says." Two bodies are in contact, but not the personalities which go with them.

Apply this same principle, now, to the relationships between boys and girls.

On this basis, petting with anybody and everybody is wrong. Why? Because under such circumstances it doesn't mean what it "says." It places two bodies in contact, but not the personalities which go with them. A kiss should mean more than heightened blood pressure, and enjoyable sensation. It should signify also some real measure of understanding and affection between two persons. But it can't possibly have this significance when a boy has picked up a strange girl on a street corner one hour ago, and now has driven with her to a nearby park. He doesn't know her. He may not even know her name. He is not acquainted with her family. He has no appreciation of the hopes, the fears, the ideals, the talents which are present within her. She is not to him a person, but only a body. And he is the same to her. Hence, if they park the car on a lonely road and wrap themselves in each other's arms, they are meeting on a purely physical level. They are playing a tune on their bodies. They are perilously close to acting out a lie, because they are using physical acts which should be the carriers of spiritual meaning —without that meaning. It might be all right for horses and cows (although they don't seem to be interested), but scarcely for human beings.

On this basis, petting by the hour is wrong. Why? Because under such circumstances it emphasizes the body too much. Imagine a wholesome couple who are right fond of each other and spend a good deal of time in each other's company. There are so many ways in which they can find mutual enjoyment.

They can swim, dance, go to the movies, skate, eat, sing, study, attend youth fellowship, or just talk. And of course they can exchange a kiss or two. Suppose now that they major on the last, slighting the others. They are impoverishing themselves and their love affair, shrinking it down to the physical alone. They are denying a large part of their true natures. They are trying to make of themselves what they are not, mere bodies. It is no wonder that such a relationship often becomes ugly, and in time turns sour. It is partial, incomplete, subhuman. No matter how pleasant it may be physically, it cannot permanently satisfy human beings. For we are bodies plus; and we get into trouble whenever we forget the "plus."

On this basis, petting which goes too far is wrong. Why? Because under such circumstances it leads to physical relationships so intimate that they are rightly reserved for life after marriage when the whole relationship between two people can be equally intimate. In home life a husband and wife can and must knit their lives together completely in every respect. They have to lay all their plans together. They have to work together in closest cooperation, each doing his share. They live together, day in and day out. They laugh at the same things, and face sorrow and difficulty side by side. If a child is ill, they stand together over his bed, and take turns sitting beside him until he recovers. In church and at home they pray together to the God and Father of us all. If now, at this stage, they share the closest possible physical intimacies, the body is not getting ahead of the procession. Instead, their physical relationship is the expression of an equally close spiritual companionship. But put these same bodily acts, or anything closely approaching them, back along the line somewhere in the period of courtship, and how different the picture becomes! The two young people cannot go all the way as yet in knitting their personal lives together. They may intend to do so some day, or they may not; but in either case, for the present it is out of the question. If, at this point, they go too far in bodily intimacies,

101

something is wrong. They are jumping the gun. They are letting the physical get ahead of the spiritual. They are acting as though they were merely or principally bodies. And that is always wrong—in industry, in international relations, in the quest for happiness, or when boy meets girl.

We have stated what is wrong in this matter of petting. On this same basis, if our fundamental principle is correct, limited physical intimacies between the sexes would be right and wholesome under certain conditions. They would be right when engaged in with a few persons, perhaps three or four at different times between puberty and engagement, for whom there is some genuine understanding and affection. They would be right when held to a subordinate place in the hours spent on dates, not usurping too much of the time. And they would be right when confined within strict limits, in accordance with a policy well thought out long before the date begins. Not too many, not too long, and not too far—these are the specific rules which grow out of a Christian philosophy of life. Some counselors with youth would draw the lines even more closely; but it is probably safe to say that a young person who follows these rules conscientiously will live normally and without regrets during his adolescent years.

One further point deserves to be mentioned. The notion has been abroad for a long time, and has been encouraged in recent years by a psychological misunderstanding, that whatever is in us ought to be expressed, and harm may result if it is not. On this theory, some people have been inclined to advocate free and full sex-expression pretty much as inner impulses dictate. But the theory itself is false! There is no necessary harm either to body or to mind in holding strong impulses temporarily in check for a good and sufficient reason. For example, if you suddenly become hungry around ten-thirty in the morning in the midst of an examination, you will suffer no injury either to body or to mind if you wait till twelve-thirty to have your dinner. You will neither get stomach ulcers, nor undergo a nervous breakdown. As a matter of fact, much of civilized life consists of refraining from doing one thing in order to do something else. This is not to say that the restraint of the impulses of either hunger or sex is easy; often it is not. But neither is it harmful. What can prove harmful is refusing to admit that these natural desires are a part of us. If we feel guilty about them and try to shove them down below the level of consciousness, then there may be trouble ahead. For thus we split ourselves in two, and the result can be a siege of worry and anxiety for which we may not know the explanation.

There is nothing shameful about sex. It is a God-given part of life. All normal persons experience its strange driving force. It is designed to join two lives in the closest union possible on this earth, and to bring new life into being. It can be read about, talked about in decency, and freely accepted as a natural, enjoyable, and beautiful part of life. But it still needs to be managed with much thought and great care. "Doing what comes naturally" makes a good song for people to sing, but not a good policy by which to run their lives.

Safety in Numbers

This means double-dating and triple-dating, going in bunches instead of by two's. It also means having a sizable number of boy friends or girl friends, and changing off from one to the other. In the twenties, there isn't much to be said for such a scheme. That is the time to narrow the field and to concentrate. But the teens are a different matter. Here there is much to favor this general policy. In fact, one of the finest books of the Bible for adolescents is the Book of Numbers!

To begin with, such a plan helps to achieve one of the main objectives of the teen-years, namely, a varied acquaintance with the opposite sex. Have you ever asked yourself what would be lost if the ten years, more or less, between puberty and marriage were wiped out, and people went straight from the one into the other? In primitive tribes, this is about what happens.

103

But with us, because of our longer period of education to fit ourselves for highly specialized vocations and our desire to have homes with furniture, rugs, and all the fixin's, a considerable period intervenes. What are these years supposed to do? So far as boy and girl relationships are concerned, their major purpose is to give young people a chance to get acquainted with different individuals and different types of the opposite sex. Without this, a person can't finally settle down to one with any assurance that he has the right one. Furthermore, he'll have to start from scratch in living well with that one.

So these are years of preparation. A boy and girl who start "going steady" with each other when they are sophomores in high school miss a great deal. They may, of course, gain something as well. Their relationship may mean much to them. And they never have to worry about what to do on Saturday night, or whom to take to a dance. But their knowledge of boys and girls in general is so limited! On the other hand, their classmates, whose affections branch out in half a dozen different directions all at once, reach the age of twenty with a considerably broader mastery of this important extracurricular subject. And the chances are they have had a better time too, as they went along.

The practice of traveling in crowds and dating in a rather hit-or-miss fashion provides a safeguard against becoming too deeply involved too soon with one person. In World War II we were told that our great danger was "too little and too late." In affairs of the heart, the danger is often just the opposite— "too much and too early." This is none too healthy, on several counts. As has been said, the couple who become wrapped up in each other at too young an age cut themselves off from a great deal. They lose the companionship of a variety of other boys and girls. They may become so completely taken up with their mutual attachment that they have little interest left for schoolwork, athletics, hobbies, or anything else. Furthermore, their relationship sometimes becomes ingrown, until they get sick and tired of the whole business and wish they hadn't started it in the first place. If it does keep fresh and wholesome, what about the years ahead? Will they finish high school; or leave to get married, and go through life handicapped by an inadequate education? Will they go on to college? Lengthy engagements are not very desirable, and often land on the rocks in one way or another. These difficulties can largely be avoided by remembering just one word—numbers. It is not a bit of magic, with the power to accomplish all good and avoid all harm. But it has much in its favor.

Multiple dating also helps to guard against the possibility of overemphasizing the physical. Heavy and prolonged petting is less likely to happen in a crowd of young people at a party or roller-skating rink than in a parlor or car occupied by two persons alone. It is also less likely to occur when the couples are reshuffled rather consistently.

Again, this same policy helps to avoid one of the twists which occur in a limited number of individuals, namely, homosexuality. The word means an emotional preference for the same sex—boys for boys, and girls for girls. It is broad enough to cover everything from a "crush" between a girl and an older woman without any physical manifestations at all, to mutual bodily stimulation by two persons of the same sex. In either case it is a dead-end street; it leads nowhere. Such a twist of the emotional life is often a highly complicated affair, with no simple cause or remedy. It may hark back to childhood in the home: a boy, for example, scared of his father; devoted to his mother; dressed in ribbons and silks; shielded from such brutal games as football; and, as a result, becoming quite effeminate, and feeling toward other boys much as a girl would. But such an outcome is less likely if, from babyhood on, the boy in question has experienced many happy and wholesome contacts with a variety of boys and girls, and now continues the same pattern in adolescence.

Once more, such a policy helps to counteract another twist,

namely, masturbation, which means getting sexual satisfaction through the stimulation of one's own body. Much of what has been written and whispered about this practice is untrue. It does not lead in most cases to either insanity or tuberculosis. A great many normal people know what the practice is from occasional (not habitual) experience. It is not the best way to live. If anything in life is meant to be shared, it is sex; and self-stimulation remains shut up within the confines of one's own life. The most important truth about it is that the practice generally represents the end-result of a good bit of loneliness, worry, and unhappiness. Therefore, one remedy lies along the lines of finding many worth-while interests in life, and reaching out to form a variety of wholesome friendships with other persons. If, from the earliest years, a child has had a reasonably happy home, and enjoyed swimming or model airplanes, and has associated all along with other boys and girls and still continues to do so in adolescence, he is not likely to take much interest in the private satisfactions of his own body.

Choosing the One and Only

The movies, the comics, and the radio are wrong a good bit of the time. They seem to imply that the chief thing necessary for choice of a life-partner is a romantic flutter of the heart, and that is it! In real life, it is not enough that the girl be good whistle-bait, and that the boy have curly hair and broad shoulders (they may be half padding anyhow). As you face this most important choice, consider these major items:

Is he (or she) attractive and desirable to me? This is by no means the place to stop in deciding upon a husband or wife, but it is perhaps the place to start. After all, you will have to look across the breakfast table at this other person a good many times. There is nothing wrong in two people being strongly and romantically drawn toward each other. The only point is that a good deal more is necessary for a successful marriage and home.

Is he (or she) emotionally grown up? The responsibilities and adjustments of home life are hard enough to meet when it is a mature man and woman facing them resolutely. They are harder, very much harder, for a boy and a girl, or a man and a girl, or a boy and a woman. So the immature person—no matter how tall, strong, or well educated—is not a good marriage risk. Such a mate will still be tied by those same old apron strings to mother or father, and will fold up and want to be babied when the going gets rough. Unless you are strong enough to carry your own share of the load, plus the other's share, plus the other person, plus several in-laws as well, think twice before linking yourself for life with someone who is decidedly and seriously immature.

Does he (or she) possess good character? This covers such positive traits as honesty, dependability, and the capacity to work steadily; and the absence of such objectionable tendencies as drinking, gambling, and a roving eye for someone else. Furthermore, it is a good rule never to expect marriage to reform a person. You may think your special case is an exception, but the odds are against you.

Does he (or she) have a cheerful, likable disposition? The honeymoon will last only a short while, and then will come the prosaic business of everyday living. How will the other person measure up to that? Have you ever seen this prospective wife on a picnic when the ants got into the sandwiches and rain washed all the make-up from her face? Or the prospective husband trying to fix a flat tire on a muddy road? A formal dance doesn't quite tell us all we need to know about the other partner in the firm.

Is he (or she) interested in religion, and in the same general type of religion as my own? Careful studies show that young people who attend Sunday school and church make better husbands and wives than those who drop out; and that there is finer harmony between parents and children in homes which practice family worship than in those which do not. Moreover, religion does its best work in a family where father and mother both belong to the same church. And if one is Protestant and the other Roman Catholic, or one Christian and the other Jewish, the actual result is likely to be less instead of more happiness. It is worth thinking about—long before the time of engagement!

Do the two of us share a good many of the same interests? The two lists need not be identical. Indeed, you may appreciate each other a bit more if one has a special talent for music, for example, and the other is an expert swimmer. Each can then view the other with wonderment and admiration; and that is a good thing. But by and large the two sets of interests should be very much alike. A husband who loves the out-of-doors and a wife who cares for nothing but bridge will have some trouble deciding how to spend their vacation; and all through the year they will lack interests which they hold in common.

The time to begin considering such questions is now. When the wedding ceremony is over, you will stand firmly pledged "from this day forward, for better for worse, for richer for poorer, in sickness and in health, to love and to cherish, till death us do part."

Man goeth forth unto his work.

9

JOBS AND VOCATIONS

Our Master toiled, a carpenter
  Of busy Galilee;
He knew the weight of ardent tasks
  And ofttimes, wearily,
He sought, apart, in earnest prayer
For strength, beneath His load of care.
He took a manly share of work,
  No thoughtless shirker He.
From dawn to dusk, before His bench,
  He labored faithfully.
He felt just pride in work well done
And found rest sweet, at setting sun.
His Father worked, and He rejoiced
  That honest toil was His—
To whom was given grace to know
  Divinest mysteries:
And shall not we find toiling good
Who serve in labor's brotherhood?

> —From "Song of Christian Workingmen,"
> by THOMAS CURTIS CLARK. Used by per-
> mission of James T. White and Com-
> pany.

HOW EASY vocational choice was, and is, in a primitive society! By and large there were only two broad classifications, men's work and women's work. No aptitude tests! No vocational counselors! No technical or professional schools! No unemployment! Nature herself made the decision into which group one should go, and that was all there was to it. During the Middle Ages in Europe the decision was almost equally simple. Girls looked forward to marriage and homemaking, and

109

that was that. Boys faced a wider range of choice, but the guild system took care of the matter quite neatly. If your father belonged to a watchmakers' guild, the presumption was that you too would become a watchmaker. So a boy merely became first an apprentice and then a craftsman in the guild to which his family belonged, and that was that. In India much the same plan has prevailed through many centuries, and down to the present time. Hindu society is divided into a number of castes and innumerable subcastes, each corresponding more or less to a certain vocation. A child, therefore, who is born into a caste of leather workers becomes a leather worker. The decision was made for him before he was born.

But in present-day America there are literally hundreds and thousands of vocations. They differ widely from one another in the training and abilities they require, as well as in other respects. Many of them are open to both men and women. No hereditary system has all the answers ready-made. So a young person must face this bewildering array of possibilities, and try to find the niche into which he will fit best during the only life which he will have on this planet. How shall he make as wise a decision as possible?

Analyzing Yourself

This is the first essential step. As you examine yourself in order to determine what sort of vocation you are best suited for, the following questions may be of some assistance:

1. *What is my general level of ability in school work?* This is not as easy to discover as might at first appear; but there are some clues pointing toward a fairly accurate answer. If you have all A's and B's on your report cards, you can probably get along in college without difficulty. Therefore a vocation which requires a college degree and perhaps postgraduate study is worth considering, if you are interested in it. On the other hand, if you have mostly C's and D's, that is another matter. There are cases, of course, where a spell of illness has dragged

a person's grades down for a semester; and others in which a boy or girl for one reason or another simply hasn't got around to consistent study. But if a high school pupil has suffered no interruptions to his work, and tried his level best without making much headway, he might well begin looking toward some vocation which does not require a higher academic education.

During recent years we have witnessed a great rush in the direction of "white-collar jobs." These were the stars to which young people hitched their wagons, and the dreams which parents cherished for their children. Several factors have been responsible for this ambition. The white-collar jobs—mostly business and the professions—have been looked up to in American society. They have seemed so easy in comparison with driving a truck or working in a steel mill (although actually they involve long hours and a good deal of nervous strain). And until the present at least they have paid more (from now on it looks as though some laborers' wages will be higher than some professional salaries). Perhaps the situation will straighten itself out in due time, but just now many young people stand a good chance of being disappointed. There simply aren't enough of these white-collar jobs to go around. Besides, some of the boys and girls who are now headed in this direction would be happier and more useful in other vocations to which they are better suited.

There is no disgrace in facing squarely the fact that a person is not well fitted for one type of work, but is admirably equipped for another. God has endowed us with different abilities, and different degrees of those abilities. The Parable of the Talents teaches clearly that he expects us to give a good account of what we have. That is all! And that is enough! Every useful occupation, we believe, is honorable in the sight of God; and it should be to us also. We can be perfectly honest, therefore, in estimating our general ability, and the vocations which best match that ability.

111

2. *What do I like most?* There are several ways to take hold of this question. What school subjects do you enjoy most? What classes do you look forward to especially? In the evening, do you pick up a math book first, and put off Latin to the very last thing? Or is it the other way around? Also, what hobbies appeal to you most? Is it reading, and, if so, what kind of reading? Or sports? Or a chemistry set? Or do you turn to your piano or trumpet whenever you get a chance? What you do in your free time affords a fairly good hint concerning the direction of your major interests.

Having said this, we must hasten to add that mere interest is not reason enough to choose a given line of work. More often than not, we are good at the same things we like. Whether we like them because we are successful in them, or whether we work hard at them because we like them, no one can say. In either case, interest and ability to some degree go hand in hand. Unfortunately, the two sometimes part company and go their separate ways. A girl may be crazy about popular music, playing it whenever a crowd gathers or even when she is alone. On the strength of this, she may conclude that music is her long suit. But when she goes to a school of music for an audition, she finds that she doesn't have the "ear," the sense of rhythm, or the muscular coordination necessary to become a talented performer. A superficial interest led her astray. On the other hand, she may not care for English, but by dint of sheer perseverance she can be good in both literature and composition—and her grades show it. This may be her real strength, and, as she works at it, her interest will awaken and grow.

3. *What can I do best?* If the foregoing is true, and it seems to be, this is a key question. And again school performance gives perhaps the best answer. Aptitude tests may help to round out the picture, but here in school is the record of what you have actually done over the years. In one school desk sits a boy with straight A's in chemistry and biology, and a nondescript assortment of other letters in French. That tells its

own story! Beside him sits another who is leading his class in mechanical drawing, but has to bone up for all he is worth to pass his history courses. That is a different story!

Some young people test out both their interests and their abilities by taking a succession of different jobs in the summer or alongside of their schoolwork. A boy may spend one summer on a farm, another in a factory, a Christmas vacation as an "extra" at the post office, and his Saturdays during one winter as a clerk in a grocery store. At the end of that time he has sampled a number of different occupations, and got some idea whether he likes them and how good he is in each one. These "tryouts" are an excellent plan; and there are other ways of making them. For example, a person could get some notion of his fitness for teaching or social work by serving as a patrol leader in a Scout troop, or a junior counselor in a summer camp for underprivileged children.

4. *Do I prefer to work with people or with things?* There is a wide difference between, let us say, a traveling salesman and a research chemist. The former has to meet people constantly. He must be able to approach them well, tell a story they haven't heard before, describe his product persuasively, and leave them happy so that he will be welcome next time. The latter spends many hours over test tubes and Bunsen burners which neither talk back nor have to be won over, but must be used with great scientific precision. Can you think of any people who would probably be a success at the one, but not at the other? In which of the two would you feel more at home?

5. *Do I prefer to carry responsibility, or let someone else make the decisions?* Some people seem to thrive on being at the center of things. They can give orders and take criticism, and not wilt under the strain. Others do not care for such front-line positions. They prefer a quiet post where they can carry out an assigned task faithfully without shouldering too much responsibility. The former group should supply the school principals and the plant superintendents; the latter, the teachers

113

and the skilled craftsmen. This is not to suggest that either one is superior to the other. They are merely different. Their life experiences to date have fitted them for separate tasks. Which type do you more nearly resemble?

Analyzing a Job

This is the second step. The following are some of the points worth considering in any prospective occupation which you have in mind:

1. *Is this job really necessary?* When transportation was difficult during the second World War, the words were frequently seen: "Is this trip really necessary?" It is a good question to ask about a job also. Does this particular occupation make a clear contribution to human welfare? Or would the world be just as well off without it? At a summer resort there are often a number of shops or booths selling trinkets. Imagine yourself operating one of these for the next forty years. You could doubtless make a good living; you might even get rich. You could conduct the business honestly, and run a decent place. On the side, it would be possible to become a good parent, church member, and citizen. But what would you be accomplishing through the job itself? Would anyone care if your shop closed down?

By way of contrast, a young woman went to Africa as a missionary nurse, but had to return home after a brief term of service because of ill health. While she was recuperating, an African chief wrote an urgent letter to her denominational mission board, telling how many mothers and babies had died since Miss S——— left them.

2. *What will twenty-five years in this job do to me?* An occupation may well be thought of as an extension of our education. Either it helps us to develop, or retards our growth, or does a little of both. Compare the probable effects upon yourself—physically, mentally, culturally, spiritually—of twenty-five years spent in each of the following:

114

Twenty-five years in a coal mine.
Twenty-five years in an office.
Twenty-five years on a farm.
Twenty-five years as a minister.
Twenty-five years beside a factory assembly-line.
Twenty-five years as a nurse.

3. *How much normal family and community life will it allow?* This point is frequently not taken into full consideration, but it deserves to be. People often think of it too late. A sales representative, for instance, may earn an excellent living in salary and commissions, and lead an interesting life. But he is away from home a good part of each week. His children grow up largely without him. He has little time to putter around the house and yard. He may get to church only occasionally. He can't plan definitely to attend a parent-teacher meeting, or canvass for the Community Chest, because he may not be at home. On the other hand, a teacher may have less money but a good many of these other things. How much do these other matters mean to you? Now is the time to think about them.

4. *How great is the demand for applicants?* Occupations obey the law of supply and demand just as automobiles, linoleum, and diamonds do. When the demand exceeds the supply in any given field, a youth stands a better chance of getting ahead in that field and receiving an adequate reward for his services. But the situation is reversed when there are many candidates competing for a limited number of positions. Then the going is hard, and the rewards often scanty. At this present moment, the need for public school teachers is greater in the elementary grades than in high school. In high school, the supply is shorter in home economics than in some other subjects. All such facts are worth looking into; and they vary greatly from time to time, and from one section of the country to another.

In some vocations there is a need for workers, but certain hurdles must be got over in order to enter the field. In medi-

115

cine, the standards for admission to an accredited medical school are quite high. In the building trades, usually a person must first be accepted as an apprentice by the labor unions. What is the situation in the occupation, or occupations, which you have in mind?

5. *What preparation is required?* If you are thinking of a job in industry, you may find employment upon graduation from high school. If you wish to rise in the ranks, a college education or even graduate work in business administration will prove invaluable. Nursing generally requires three years after high school; the ministry, seven; medicine, eight or so; teaching, four; a college professorship, a master's degree and preferably a Ph.D.; secretarial work, a much shorter course in a business school. You can be a farmer without extra training, but a degree from a school of agriculture will enable you to be a much better farmer. And thus it goes around the circle.

6. *How much capital is needed to get started?* A laborer in industry can make a start with merely his hands and his head; nothing more! A dentist, on the contrary, needs office equipment running into a good many hundreds of dollars. A sizable farm costs in the thousands or tens of thousands. How much would it be for a garage mechanic? A garage operator? A laboratory technician? A public accountant? A civil engineer? A social worker?

7. *What is the promotion-ladder?* Occupations differ widely in the number of rungs between the bottom and the top, and the distances between the rungs. Suppose, for example, that you are thinking of teaching in the public school system. You can easily find out your approximate starting salary. Then there is probably in your state a definite plan of upgrading according to the number of years taught and the amount of postgraduate work done. Beyond that lie such positions as school principal or superintendent, if you are interested in administration. The lowest rung isn't too low, and the highest isn't too high; and the whole ladder can be pictured fairly well. But suppose your

aim is to be a concert pianist. Either you make it, or you don't. At the bottom, you might find it impossible to support yourself through your playing, and have to turn to other work. At the top, there are fabulous salaries; but only a few land there, and they remain a good while. In between there isn't too much: a job as accompanist, or a spot on a radio program, but nothing very sure. How is it with the occupations that appeal to you?

8. *How much money will I make?* This is the question often asked first of all, but it is placed last in the present list. It really doesn't deserve to be put first. Money is a very useful commodity. Everyone needs some. It would be foolish not to inquire whether a given job is likely to provide the means for a comfortable and happy life. But it is equally foolish to let the dollar mark loom so large as to shut out some of these other considerations.

A certain college was in dire need of a professor of physics, at a time when such teachers were as scarce as hen's teeth. An approach was made to a man with thorough training and long teaching experience, who was at the moment employed in industry. The best salary the college could offer was far below what the industry was paying. The man found he would be slicing his salary exactly in half if he made the change. For a while he wasn't sure he could do it, but then he decided in favor of teaching. In explaining his decision, he said: "When the accounts are all in, I believe I would rather look back upon a life spent with people than upon one spent with gadgets." Money is something, but it isn't everything.

Putting the Two Together

This is the third step. First, you appraise yourself as honestly as you can. Then you learn about as many jobs as possible, narrow these down to a few, and study them intensively. Then you match the two sets of findings, and see where you come out. This is the process of vocational choice, boiled down to its essentials.

117

Tests of interest or aptitude may be of real help at one point or another along the line. The Gentry Vocational Inventory, which can be procured at 3433 Walnut Street, Philadelphia 4, Pennsylvania, is a good one. A word of caution must be said at this point. You really need the help of an experienced vocational counselor in interpreting the results of this or any other such test. Otherwise you may draw the wrong conclusions, and get off on the wrong track. Many public schools and social agencies nowadays contain people who have had specialized training in this field, and might be willing to confer with an individual or meet with a youth group.

Several other words of caution are in order also.

It is not true that out of the thousands of occupations there is only one which is suitable for any given person. This is as false as the mistaken assumption that out of the thousands of girls in the world one particular girl is meant for a certain boy, or one particular boy for a certain girl. What is true—to come back to vocations—is that one type or "family" of vocations may be much more suitable for the individual in question than another. To illustrate, one person might be almost equally happy as a social worker, a teacher, or a minister. Another might make out almost equally well as an accountant, an instructor of mathematics, or a bank clerk. But neither could switch easily to the opposite grouping.

It is not true that young people "owe it to their parents" to allow father and mother to choose their vocations for them. Much unhappiness has arisen in the vain attempt of young men and women to fit into a niche all cut out for them by parental wishes, but in which they had little or no interest. What is true is that we ought to consider seriously our parents' wishes, their judgment, their ideals, their standards. But the ultimate decision must be made by each individual himself. He is the one who will have to work at the job. He should have the privilege and accept the responsibility of deciding what it is to be.

118

Finally, what is a girl to do with her life? She faces a problem which does not trouble her brother, namely, "Shall I follow the time-honored vocation of homemaker and mother, or aim at some position in the business and professional world?" There is a third option—to try to do both. Some women, with careful planning, are following this course successfully. No definite answer can be given which will fit all cases. But one thing is sure: the vocation of homemaker and mother is as honorable as any under the sun. These words are being written in the year of a nation-wide United States Census. We may safely guess that more than one woman will greet the census taker at the door, and, wiping her hands on her apron, give her occupation as "only a housewife." The word "only" should be stricken from the record.

Where Does Religion Come In?

Too often it doesn't. Several studies have been made which show that many young people don't seem to take their religious convictions into conscious consideration at all in the midst of choosing a job. The two remain in separate compartments with little or no effect on each other.

This is a strange circumstance indeed. For Christian faith holds that all our talents of body and mind come from God, and are to be used in his service. They are not ours; they are his. They are placed in our keeping, but they belong to Someone beyond ourselves. Surely this is something to think of when it comes to choosing a vocation. Or, to say it differently, our Christian faith plainly teaches that each person finds his highest fulfillment in doing God's will, as he understands it. If he sets out to follow his own little private ambitions, he is doomed to unhappiness and failure, no matter how "successful" he may be in the usual sense of the word. But if he tries to fathom God's purpose for all life and make that purpose his own, the joy and satisfaction he achieves will be greater than he would have dreamed possible.

119

We need, therefore, to recapture the original sense of the word "vocation." It means literally a "calling." And who does the calling? There is only one answer, namely, God.

Every Christian youth, then, ought to be able to feel that he is called of God to the lifework which he undertakes. This does not as a rule imply any dream, or vision, or mysterious experience. Most of us discover God's will for our lives in very ordinary ways. We can think about the matter as clearly as we know how. We can talk it over with some trusted friend and counselor. We can also pray about it in the spirit of obedient search for the way we ought to go. If, at the end of such a process, we find something that needs to be done, that benefits God's people and advances his kingdom, and for which we are reasonably well qualified, we are entitled to feel that God has called us to that lifework. A banker who selects his profession in this way, and tries to follow it in the same manner, can say truthfully that he believes himself to be called of God to be a banker. He is in full-time Christian service. So is a farmer under like conditions, a nurse, a steelworker, a housewife, a butcher, or a missionary. The world desperately needs men and women in every useful vocation who will view their work in this light, and act accordingly.

The world also needs an increasing number of capable, likable young men and women who will give serious consideration to the so-called church vocations. There are so many of them nowadays! We used to think of only two—minister and missionary. But now we have, in addition to the general ministry, directors of Christian education, ministers of music, hospital chaplains, rural work specialists, urban work specialists, church social workers, student pastors, teachers in church-related institutions, denominational and interdenominational executives, and many others. On the mission field at home and abroad we have evangelistic missionaries, educational missionaries, medical missionaries, agricultural missionaries, economists, audiovisual technicians, and many others. All of them are employed by the Church, and have devoted their lives to the service of mankind through the Church. In fact, it would be hard to name any constructive ability which cannot be used by the Christian Church in its manifold activities today.

This is not to say that every boy or girl who is earnestly trying to reach a Christian decision should enter one of these church vocations. That would upset our national life, for we would run short of bankers, farmers, laborers, and everything else. Besides, not all young people are equally fitted for professional service in and through the Church. Some of them will be happier and more useful elsewhere. And, as we have said, every worthy vocation is a calling from God. But the need is so great that no capable Christian youth ought to reach a decision on his lifework without having given one good, long, honest, earnest look at the possibility of investing his life in some corner of the Church's far-flung program.

Teach me thy way, O Lord.

—PSALM 86: 11

10

FINDING A WAY OF LIFE

To every man there openeth
A Way, and Ways, and a Way,
And the High Soul climbs the High Way,
And the Low Soul gropes the Low,
And in between on the misty flats,
The rest drift to and fro.
But to every man there openeth
A High Way and a Low,
And every man decideth
The Way his soul shall go.

—From *Gentlemen—The King!*, by JOHN
OXENHAM. The Pilgrim Press. Used by
permission.

YOUTH is the time above all others for the making of
crucial decisions. Three in particular belong to this period:
first, choosing a life-partner; second, choosing a life-work; and
third, choosing a life-philosophy, or a way of life. None of
these is made in childhood, for that would be too early. Except
in unusual circumstances, none is put off until adulthood, for
that would be too late. But each of them must be faced by
young people.

Of these three, the last is probably the most important, for
the reason that it has much to do with the other two. In select-
ing "the one and only" a person shows clearly in what order
he ranks beauty, brains, character, disposition, and the like. In
other words, he reveals the way of life he has adopted for his
own. Likewise in deciding upon a vocation a person places
salary ahead of service, or home life above fame and fortune,

and thus tips his hand concerning his way of life. So the third choice mentioned is fundamental.

Some adolescents simply drift into a way of life, without giving the matter much thought. They will play records by the hour to select the ones they want to buy, or try on clothes until the clerks are exhausted; but they "ooze" unconsciously into the most important selection of all. Others get into the wrong way, and bring heartaches upon themselves, their parents, and their friends. But a great many find the high way, and grow stronger and finer as the years come and go.

Everyone Has His Own

A newspaper account tells of a man in a small town who habitually "went out with the boys" and drank heavily. One evening he came home with his senses and judgment dulled by liquor, and began to beat his wife. Her father, who was nearby, came to her rescue armed with a gun. When it was all over, the father-in-law had shot the husband and killed him. A widowed mother must now rear her family as best she can. Several children will grow up lacking a normal home life, and perhaps deprived of the education they might otherwise have received. The father-in-law carries the memory of shooting and killing another. All because a man had a way of life! The chances are that he never gave five minutes of serious thought to the issue; at least, the outcome would so suggest. If a neighbor had met him one day and asked, "What is your philosophy of life?" he would probably have been speechless—or worse. But he had a way of life.

A few years ago a child movie star was the delight of all who saw her pictures. She was sweet, unspoiled, and talented. Everyone loved her, and wished her well. She grew up in the spotlight of popularity, and in the midst of wealth and luxury. Now she has divorced her second husband. She has a way of life.

For some time a scientist in an eastern university has quietly been conducting researches in his laboratory. America is his adopted home, for he came to our shores as an immigrant from another country. Not long ago he discovered a miracle-working drug which will be of inestimable benefit to mankind. Diseases which were formerly incurable will now respond to treatment. People who would otherwise have died will now continue to live. He could have sold his discovery for a small fortune, salting it away for himself. Instead he has chosen to turn the proceeds over to the institution where he teaches. And so he goes on lecturing and experimenting, not wealthy but quite content with his lot. He has a way of life.

Nineteen centuries have elapsed since a young man labored at a carpenter bench in the little town of Nazareth. His work was hard, for there were many mouths to feed. His home was humble, and his clothes plain. His pleasures were few—chiefly the companionship of family and friends, the beauty of the lilies at his feet and the birds over his head, the worship and rest of the Sabbath day, and perhaps the occasional excitement of a caravan train or a troop of Roman soldiers riding by. With it all, he was strangely sensitive to God's will and God's love. In his early thirties he left home and shop, and gave himself without reserve for two brief years to preaching, teaching, and healing. He held no shares in any company; owned no real estate; never drove an automobile, saw a movie, or listened to a radio. And yet he spoke a great deal about joy. When he was midway in his allotted threescore years and ten, he was crucified on a stark hill between two thieves—and is alive forevermore. He too had a way of life. To countless numbers of his followers he has become the way, the truth, and the life.

What Is Yours?

Whether you have thought much about it or not, you have a way of life. It goes with you wherever you go. You cannot take it off like an overcoat, and hang it in a closet. It shapes your decisions, and guides your actions. It helps to make you

124

what you are now, and to determine what you will become in the years ahead. It is like a tapestry into which are woven the threads of all you have experienced thus far. Nothing that you have ever done, or that has ever happened to you, is left out. Home, school, church, playground, friends, successes, failures —they are all there. Presumably on more than one occasion you have lifted it up and examined it with some care. This may have occurred at a summer camp, during your private prayers, or in a discussion group at church. If so, it has been polished a little, and the rough edges smoothed off.

What is your way of life? How can you tell? Here are some fairly dependable clues:

The way you spend your time. If you have never kept an exact record for a week, you might find it worth your while. There are one hundred and sixty-eight hours in seven days. If we allow fifty-six hours for sleep, thirty hours for school, and twelve hours for meals, this leaves seventy hours a week at your own disposal more or less. How many of these do you devote to study? To recreation? To helping around the home? To work for which you get paid? To church? To loafing? The answers reflect your way of life.

The use you make of your money. You may have much or little. Perhaps you earn some for yourself, or depend entirely upon an allowance. But where does it go? Again, if you have never kept a strict account, you might care to do so for a month. How much of it goes for clothes? Books? A good time? High school lunches? Music? Church? Articles in a store window that strike your eye, such as a ball-point pen or a piece of jewelry? Savings for college? If you have to choose between a movie and a contribution to European or Asiatic relief, which wins out?

The things you enjoy most. Compare, for example, your feelings toward a major high school dance and a particularly impressive communion service. To which do you look forward with keener anticipation? Which gives you the greater satisfaction while it is going on? Which do you remember the longer? (This is a rather severe test. It is not meant to imply that there is anything wrong about enjoying a dance to the full. It does serve as a mirror in which a person can see himself as he truly is at the moment.) In the same manner, set the following over against one another: the rough-and-tumble of a basketball game; an opera; a box of choice chocolates; a hike through the hills on an autumn day; a romantic date; a stimulating book; a chance to settle an old account with an enemy.

The people you admire. For purposes of admiration, we generally select persons who embody the qualities that appeal to us most. Hence your list of "idols" is another reasonably good indication of the way of life which you are following. Who are on your list? Betty Grable? Frank Sinatra? Albert Schweitzer? Abraham Lincoln? Joe DiMaggio? Winston Churchill? Jane Addams? People known to you in your own community? A series of names such as this is soon outdated in part, but the principle remains the same. You can always discover something about yourself from the kind of person you admire.

The things you are willing to work for. There is an old maxim that, no matter how busy we may be, we always find time and energy for anything we really want. A football player spends many grueling afternoons and gives up dates and sundaes in order to make the team and have a successful season. Nobody could make him do it. He does it because it represents something he wants, something that is a part of him and his way of life. A student studying for honors; an actor in a dramatic production; a musician practicing for a recital; a member of a committee decorating the gymnasium for a big dance— each does the same. And each, in so doing, reveals something about his way of life. What do you find yourself willing to work for?

The picture you cherish of yourself ten years from now. What is the chief item in that picture? It may be marriage and a home. Or maybe you dream of rising to the top in your chosen profession, and seeing your name in the newspaper headlines. Or perhaps it is wealth, with a solid house in a swanky residential section, membership in the country club, and all the rest. It might be bigger and better convertibles, horse races, and night clubs. Or at the center of the picture you may see yourself giving some boy or girl a chance you never had. Whatever it is, it can tell you a good deal about yourself now.

The foregoing are six clues to your real way of life, not what you think it is, or wish it were, but what it actually is. Others could be added, such as the manner in which you view other people—as handy articles to have around when you want money or a date or some favor, or as persons who are to be treated with respect and consideration; the way you manage yourself—giving in to every little whim, or running things with a firm hand; and the way you react to difficulty—shying off in self-pity, or getting your back up and trying it again. But the list is probably long enough. It opens the door for about as much self-examination as is wholesome at any one time.

In the light of these probing questions, how would you describe your way of life? If you had to put it into words, what would they be? Is it a good way? Is it the best way? How close is it to *the* way as embodied in Jesus?

If what you find does not satisfy you altogether, it can be changed. Not all at once, of course; but little by little it will respond to thoughtful, earnest effort. We do have some control over our lives. Within limits we can head them in the direction in which they ought to go. But we do not accomplish this best by concentrating long on ourselves. Our best bet is to point our lives toward something outside ourselves—something to live for, and something to live by.

Something Big to Live For

Everyone needs this. Conceivably a dog or a fox can get along without it, but not a human being. With our ability not only to live in the present hour but also to look ahead toward

127

the future, we must have something to live for. Otherwise, life loses much of its meaning.

The biggest possible thing to live for is the will of God.

An instructor of religion in a boys' preparatory school used to follow a unique procedure in introducing his subject. On the blackboard he would draw a time-line representing the past ten thousand years. This he would mark off into periods, as a ruler is divided into inches. Then with the class he would trace man's slow and painful ascent out of the caves and jungles into civilization. One by one they listed the major inventions, extending from such early discoveries as the use of iron to modern discoveries like steam and electricity. Entered also at the proper place were the tours of exploration of Marco Polo, Christopher Columbus, and others, which gradually covered the globe and gave men knowledge of one world. Alongside of this, they placed the social progress of mankind from smaller to ever larger units of organization—first the clan, then the tribe, the city-state, the nation, and finally a single global civilization. Naturally they listed in order the rise and fall of nations, beginning with Egypt and Babylonia, and running through Greece and Rome down to Spain, France, England, and the United States. Then they got to the heart of the matter. Along that line they saw the human race making its painful way, with many lapses, upward from heartless cruelty to heartfelt sympathy. First, all captives in war were tortured and killed. Then some were spared to become slaves. Then slavery itself was attacked, and outlawed. Now we still have war, but we are trying to humanize it, and hoping even to do away with it. To begin with, new-born babies were buried alive if they were not wanted, or abandoned to be picked up by anyone who could raise them for his own selfish advantage. In time the conscience of humanity revolted against such barbarism, and childhood was cherished and protected. Now in many nations huge sums of money are spent to educate children, fix their teeth, and feed them vitamins. In the first stage, a person was justified in killing anyone who harmed him in the least. Then revenge was whittled down to match precisely the injury: "an eye for an eye, and a tooth for a tooth." At long last, we reached the ideal (although we don't always practice it) of loving our enemies and returning good for evil.

When this tremendous story of mankind was finally unrolled before their eyes, the instructor would quietly say: "There is God's will for this planet. There is his plan for his children. The scene before you is the tedious growth of his kingdom. What still lies ahead in the future? And where do you fit in? What can you do to help this process along? What vocation can you follow that will carry this development to higher levels?" This is what we mean by living for the will of God.

Such a purpose will influence everything a person does. Not only will it enter into his choice of a lifework, but it will creep also into his actions at home, on a date, or out with the gang. He will try so to act as to push that line onward and upward. The way he spends his money, the use he makes of his time, the attitude he takes toward Negroes—all will be affected. He may not talk much about it, but it will be the master motive of his life.

Such a purpose gives point and meaning to life. Have you ever put in hours preparing for something like a school play, working day and night up to the moment of the final curtain, and then felt let down the next morning? All dressed up and no place to go! Nothing to work for! Nothing to live for! While the rehearsals were going on, you doubtless fussed and fumed about it, but at least life was interesting. But when it was over —then the bottom dropped out of everything. The person who lives for the will of God is never let down. He always has something ahead, something big, something worth striving for, something that makes life worth living.

Such a purpose also helps to free a person from painful self-consciousness. It gets his mind off himself. It saves him from worrying all the time about his blood pressure, his popularity,

129

his looks, his own future, and what other people say about him. You see, such things don't matter greatly, if one has something big "out there" to live for. They are trivial. The thing that matters is what happens to that line. And so the seeker for the kingdom is blissfully unaware of himself, and enjoys a happiness which others don't know.

It is clear, then, that one major secret of continuous personal growth is simply to live wholeheartedly for the accomplishment of God's will among men. One time Peter, who never hesitated to ask questions, inquired of Jesus what rewards would come to those who left everything and followed him. The answer is very strange. "Jesus said, Truly I say to you, there is no one who has left house or brothers or sisters or mother or father or children or lands, for my sake and for the gospel, who will not receive a hundredfold now in this time, houses and brothers and sisters and mothers and children and lands, with persecutions, and in the age to come eternal life." We completely miss the point of these verses (Mark 10: 29-30) if we insist on taking them too literally. Jesus couldn't have meant that a disciple would receive a hundred houses for every one he gave up, or a hundred mothers. Rather he seems to have been assuring them that anyone who gives up some things to follow him in doing the will of God will be repaid a hundred times over in happiness and richness of life, with some persecution scattered along the way, and this happiness and spiritual richness will go on forever. That is true! It was so then, and it is so now. Many have experienced it for themselves, and you can also.

Something Sure to Live By

Everyone needs this. An elephant or a hummingbird can possibly get along without it, but not a human being. For we remember yesterday's hurts so long, and feel today's so keenly, that we must have something to live by. Without something sure to depend upon, life may become almost unbearable.

The surest possible thing to live by is the love of God.

A few years ago the vesper hill of one of our summer camps was the scene of a marriage service. This is a spot with many precious associations for young people who have attended the camp. The approach to it is a lane flanked by evergreen trees. From the top of the hill, one may look far across a peaceful valley to a notch in the hills on the horizon. The bride had come to know and love this place, and wished to be married there. Since it was wartime, the groom wore the uniform of the United States Navy. He was then on terminal leave, which meant that soon after his return to duty he would sail for one of the combat areas. Where he was going, he did not know. When he would get back, he did not know. Whether he would return at all, he could not say. And neither could she! It was a solemn moment when the couple took their marriage vows on this hilltop, with the future so insecure and perilous. When the service was finished, the bride turned to the minister and said: "If it were not for my faith in God, I think I could not go through this."

That is the point exactly. Time and again we come to crises which we could scarcely go through—except for our faith in God's never failing love toward us. For we are such little creatures. We stand only five or six feet tall, tiny specks on the surface of a planet spinning endlessly in an enormous universe. Our bodies live only a short while, as time goes. And during their brief span of life they are attacked by germs and viruses, and subject to accidents which tear the flesh and break the bones. Our spirits too are open to many sorts of injury. A chance remark cuts us to the quick. We run for office, and are defeated. We apply for a job, and don't get it. We fall in love, and are disappointed. Those who are near and dear to us make mistakes, bringing disgrace upon the family circle. Sickness, accident, poverty, shame, defeat, anxiety, and death—all of these walk near our sides. We may avoid them for a while, but sooner or later one falls in step and becomes our companion. Or it may be two or three of them at a time.

131

In addition, there is the common experience of doing something wrong, so wrong that we hardly know how to hold our heads up again. Sometimes we blame ourselves unjustly, but in other instances there can be no question about our failure. Then we labor under a sense of guilt, which weighs upon us like a heavy burden. We cannot look others squarely in the face. And we hesitate even to look directly at ourselves.

In all such experiences of sorrow and sin, we need the assurance of God's love to live by. St. Paul went through enough trouble to crush a person of weaker faith. He tells us about it in II Corinthians 11: 24-27: "Five times I have received at the hands of the Jews the forty lashes less one. Three times I have been beaten with rods; once I was stoned. Three times I have been shipwrecked; a night and a day I have been adrift at sea; on frequent journeys, in danger from rivers, danger from robbers, danger from my own people, danger from Gentiles, danger in the city, danger in the wilderness, danger at sea, danger from false brethren; in toil and hardship, through many a sleepless night, in hunger and thirst, often without food, in cold and exposure." And what was it that carried him through triumphantly? He tells us that too: "We know that in everything God works for good with those who love him" (Romans 8: 28).

Such a faith holds a person steady in the midst of all difficulties. God does not save us or those we love from pain and suffering. Nor can he keep the nations of the world from throwing mankind into war, if they insist on disobeying his will. But he does walk beside us every step of the way. He knows that we are suffering, and suffers with us. Furthermore, no harm—real harm, that is—can come to any of us; even death itself is merely an incident, and a change of residence, as it were. We remain within the Father's keeping. And perhaps these trials will actually work out for good in ways now hidden to us.

Such a faith lifts a person up when he is bowed down by a sense of guilt. For no matter what we have done, God's forgiveness is ours for the asking if we turn to him with childlike trust

FINDING A WAY OF LIFE

and a firm intent to follow his will more closely in the future than in the past. He can not undo the harm we may have done, but he receives us with open arms, takes our shame away, and helps us set our feet once more in the path of goodness and decency.

It is clear, then, that a major secret of continuous personal growth is simply to live daily by the assurance of God's unchanging love. The everlasting arms are beneath us at all times. There is nothing to worry about in the past, the present, or the future—absolutely nothing! This is almost too good to be true, but it is true. If we do the best we can, the rest is in God's hands. He will take care of it. And we can go through life with the calm poise and trust so beautifully expressed in the lines of Whittier:

> I know not where His islands lift
> Their fronded palms in air;
> I only know I cannot drift
> Beyond His love and care.
> And Thou, O Lord, by whom are seen
> Thy creatures as they be,
> Forgive me if too close I lean
> My human heart on Thee.